BORN GRAY IN A BLACK AND WHITE WORLD
WADE OLIVER

authorHOUSE

AuthorHouse™
1663 Liberty Drive
Bloomington, IN 47403
www.authorhouse.com
Phone: 1-800-839-8640

© 2010 Wade Oliver. All rights reserved.

No part of this book may be reproduced, stored in a retrieval system, or transmitted by any means without the written permission of the author.

First published by AuthorHouse 12/15/2010

ISBN: 978-1-4520-9408-3 (sc)
ISBN: 978-1-4520-9409-0 (dj)
ISBN: 978-1-4520-9410-6 (e)

Library of Congress Control Number: 2010916688

Printed in the United States of America

Any people depicted in stock imagery provided by Thinkstock are models, and such images are being used for illustrative purposes only. Certain stock imagery © Thinkstock.

This book is printed on acid-free paper.

Cover design by Patrick Weld
http:/www.patrickweld.com

Because of the dynamic nature of the Internet, any Web addresses or links contained in this book may have changed since publication and may no longer be valid. The views expressed in this work are solely those of the author and do not necessarily reflect the views of the publisher, and the publisher hereby disclaims any responsibility for them.

This book would not be possible without divine love from the twin French brothers; Clemence and Faveur. Together they have given me more than I deserved and have protected me from the just do consequences I should have received. I also say thanks to Anthony my guardian Angel. I figure it is about time to give you a name.

TABLE OF CONTENTS

Foreward ix
Chapter 1 Fearfully & Wonderfully Made 1
Chapter 2 Dropped at the Curb 6
Chapter 3 FrankenDad 14
Chapter 4 UFO's, Police Chases, and Car Crashes 23
Chapter 5 Trouble with a Smile 29
Chapter 6 Flying Bananas 34
Chapter 7 My Best Friend the Plant 42
Chapter 8 Wasted Opportunity- The School Years 51
Chapter 9 If Uncle Sam only Knew 59
Chapter 10 Colonel Makes a Promise 67
Chapter 11 Nine Lives Minus Eight 73
Chapter 12 The Cat is Dead 80
Chapter 13 Amazing Grace 90
Chapter 14 The Girl from Siam 96
Chapter 15 Marriage and the Angel 102
Chapter 16 Barney and the Power Rangers 107
Chapter 17 Delana and the Demon 117
Chapter 18 Divorce and Remarriage 122
Chapter 19 God's House 130
Chapter 20 Aliens at the Post Office 138
Chapter 21 Full Circle 149
Conclusion 157

FOREWARD

I did not wake up everyday looking in the mirror feeling disconnected from humanity, but I had moments when I felt like the Lone Ranger. While others were excitingly celebrating their annual group heritage festivals and paying homage to famous kin, I had a spirit of apathy during black history month, St. Patrick's Day and anything related to my English, and Russian Jewish ancestry. All were pieces of the puzzle that made up my existence, but in a confused and self-protective way I chose to rejoice in none of them so as to not dishonor the others. I was trying to maintain equality within the League of Nations that I represented.

In the world's naturally divisive way, value tags are pinned on to people based upon their race, social and economic status. The last two were easy enough to figure out as I was a social Joe Blow suburban kid clinging onto the lower rungs of the prosperity ladder. It was the first one I was cloudy about. Whose team was I on, or could I be on more than one team at the same time? I accepted that I was caught in the middle of two worlds; a blend so to speak, and that blend was **GRAY**. Later as a young adult my phone rang and the person on the other end asked to speak to 'Mr. Empty'. I told him I was he. He told me that I was floundering and would be **GRAY** in spirit forever until I understood who he is, who I am and what my purpose is. The conversation lasted many days and ended when he told me about the universal truth that was spoken to a man in the cloak of night named Nicodemus almost two thousand years ago.

If you are Gray or in my case a double Gray this book is for you. If you are any other color you are welcome to read as well. Just put on your seat belt because the ride will take you through the valley of bewilderment, tunnel of sadness and the many hills of laughter until you reach the mountain of Joy.

Here is my story.

CHAPTER 1

Fearfully & Wonderfully Made

"For you formed my inward parts; you covered me in my mother's womb. I will praise you, for I am fearfully and wonderfully made; marvelous are your works, and that my soul knows very well. My frame was not hidden from you, when I was made in secret. And in Your book they all were written, the days fashioned for me, when as yet there were none of them." (Psalm 139:13-16)

My story begins on a gray winter day in January 1965. To be exact, the date was the eighteenth and it was a cold day in Minneapolis Minnesota. My surroundings were pretty much the same as most babies born in a hospital: warm incubator, smiling nurses, and a baby mobile hanging from the crib. I don't remember this; it's just what I would expect based on the numerous movies I have seen. I was a cute baby, but then the aging process took over and my best days were behind me. I looked like little Ricky Ricardo and my mother said I was a happy little tyke. The *happy* has fortunately remained, but the little tyke has grown into a double cheeseburger and fries too many around the mid-section. Before continuing in the forward direction of time, I need to go back a few years. This will bring some clarity and understanding into my story.

There are many influences that go into molding a child into the gray life. The obvious and most important of those influences are your mother and father. My mother was and is a caring and loving mother. What she lacked in wisdom she made up for in love. I remember never going hungry, being without shelter, or being unloved. My mother has been plagued with emotional problems most of her life. Some, I believe are a direct result of growing up in a household where she received less than the needed amount of nurturing and teaching.

Because my mother lives in the deep gray, her life has been a series of ups and downs, with most of it spent in the valleys of despair. Like most parents including myself, we all look back and recognize we missed the bulls-eye and landed our parenting in the outer circles and in some cases we missed the target altogether. In our conversations over the years, my mom has shared with me how she regrets her poor decisions, but is relieved that her two sons have turned out all right in spite of her missteps. I would have to agree with her.

My mother was born on November 1, 1940 in Minneapolis Minnesota. She was born into a Jewish home in the Jewish community of North Minneapolis. Franklin Delano Roosevelt was president of the United States serving in his eighth year of office. On the other side of the globe, a madman named Adolph Hitler was demonically manipulating and inspiring the most powerful army in the world to storm Europe. His grandiose intent was world domination and extermination of the Jewish race. My mother met my father somewhere in the neighborhood of 1960-61. He was the first man who ever gave her real attention and said all of the things that a woman wants to and should hear. It would take her many years before she understood and accepted that this man who was saying all of the right things was actually a wolf, concerned only with satisfying his lustful desires. From here on the relationship becomes a "what-not-to-do guide to relationships." Harvey is his name, and he was seven years my mother's senior. Sometime later, Harvey would become the first black ambulance driver in the state of Minnesota.

My mother and Harvey began an intimate relationship while Harvey was still married and raising three little girls. Mother's family was justifiably very unhappy about this relationship with a married man. What compounded this and made it more unappealing was the social taboo being violated. Harvey was a black man. America at this time was still resistant towards the union of interracial couples, and many states still had anti-miscegenation laws that prohibited marriage or sexual activity of any person of African descent to another person who was not of African descent. "The all men are created equal" in the Declaration of Independence had excluded the darker offspring of Adam and Eve. In 1967, the Supreme Court wisely reversed these laws.

My mother had a fragile relationship with her siblings and mother, and the relationship she had with Harvey made it even more brittle. She became the figurative black sheep of the family and my brother and I (both of us not yet born) would become real-life living and breathing black lambs. In the first eighteen years of life I remember visiting her brother and sisters a total of about six times. At no time do I remember them ever coming over to visit our house or apartment. Besides my two aunts, uncle and grandma, my mother had no contact with the few relatives she had, and thus, I never met them, whoever they were.

Harvey's side of the family was much larger. With the exception of one event that entailed going up to his lake cabin, I remember nothing about any of my paternal blood relations I may have been introduced to except Aunt Mattie. When my stepdad would come on the scene, the twenty or so times that I went to his family's side were generally without Mom and Cory. They were all very nice and they all embraced me like I was a blood relative who had been apart of the family from the beginning, but I felt like an outsider.

The bomb blew up and the proverbial "last straw" took place in Mom's family when everyone found out that she was pregnant with me. This caused the cohabitation of my grandmother, Aunt Jean (who passed away in the 1970s from cancer), her son Scott, my uncle, my youngest aunt, and my mother to disband from the small duplex that they shared.

Mom told me she had no self-esteem, was immature and insecure and that she was in love with Harvey. I have read books and have listened to pastors and bible teachers such as James Dobson who have said that if a young girl does not receive the proper love and affirmation from her father, the odds increase that she will find it in such ways as my mother did. My mother told me she has no memory of her father ever giving her a hug and has only one sweet memory of him when she was sitting on his lap one time. My grandfather was involved in an affair with another woman and was absent emotionally from his wife and my mom for many years, if not most. He died in 1955 when my mother was fourteen years old.

After refusing the advice to abort me (thanks mom), in August of 1964 at the age of 23, she went to the Booth home for unwed mothers in St. Paul. No one knew what to do to help her and believed it was in everyone's best interest if she went there. She was four months pregnant and shipped off to become someone else's problem. She slept in her own bed in a giant community room with about fifty other young girls and women who were unmarried and pregnant. My mother was given the daily job of cleaning the delivery and recovery room. This involved cleaning up all of the blood and afterbirth.

In September about five weeks in her stay, she went to the local drugstore and purchased a bottle of aspirin. She swallowed many of the aspirin and then went back to the Booth Home. After a short period of time she told the person in charge what she did and they immediately contacted the University of Minnesota Hospital. She was taken and admitted into the locked ward of the psychiatric unit. Sadly my mother in her bouts of depression would do this a few more times in her adult life. This instance as with the other feeble attempts that would occur in the future were never with the intention of true suicide but were an escape from reality and the consequences of her actions into the confines of a safe haven that temporarily gave her respite.

After a couple of weeks of observation and assessments they moved her to the open psych ward unit. My mother remained in that unit until I was born. She was the only patient who was pregnant. Hours before I was born my mother's water broke. Since she felt good and nothing seemed to be happening she went to dinner. After dinner she stopped and asked one of the nurses casually what is the next stage after your water breaks. The nurse looked at her puzzled and asked her why? Mom told her that her water broke before dinner and she was just wondering. The nurse made a call and then they wheeled her into labor and sometime after that I was born.

A couple days after my birth, someone in the hospital staff came and told my mom that they had taken me and placed me into a foster home. Mom said she went hysterical. Everyone assumed that she was going to give me up for adoption. They unilaterally made the decision without conversing with her to see what her plans were for providing for herself and a new baby. After repeatedly declaring that she was not going to give me up, the authorities relinquished their initial position and said it would only be temporary if she met one condition. She would have to get her own place, and this was something she had never had before. As my mom was telling me this story in the living room of her apartment, she began to cry.

What if my mom would have let me go? Would I have ever been adopted into a loving family, or would I have been like so many boys and girls in the foster home world who would be bounced to and fro never experiencing the bond of at least one person who was there unconditionally for them? To know that there are so many kids out there who have no mother and father is horrible. To know that I am selfish and afraid to look into becoming a foster parent makes me ashamed to one day stand before God. Maybe one day that will change.

Two weeks after I was born my mother left the hospital and her

Aunt and Uncle opened up their house in Brooklyn Park for her to live. Everyday she would get on a bus and travel down to the house where the foster family was caring for me. It was very hard for her when she left, but it motivated her to work that much harder to find a place of her own. A couple weeks later she found a place for the two of us. She called Harvey to help her move a few of her possessions into the North Minneapolis house where she was going to rent a room. This would be the first time Harvey had seen me. To his credit, he said this place was not fit for the two of us and helped us find another place to live. This was the beginning of my gypsy life style.

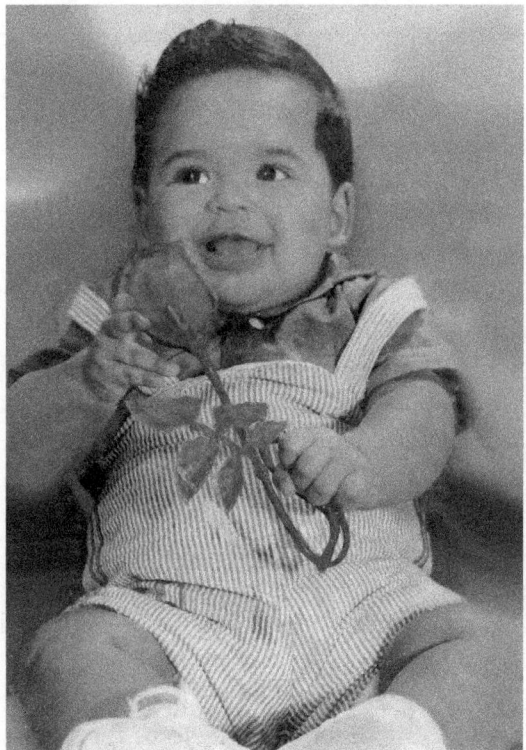

Little Wade

CHAPTER 2

Dropped at the Curb

My earliest memory in life is the eighth or ninth of April 1968. My mother was at the hospital giving birth to her and Harvey's second child together and my soon to be little brother. I was staying at Harvey's aunt's house for the two days that my mom was at the hospital. Aunt Mattie was her name and my mom said she was the only person in Harvey's family who showed her any love. I understand the distancing and resentment that existed towards my mother, me and my soon to be born little brother. It takes two to tango and my mother was a willing participant in this unholy union. Besides the nature of the relationship, the other woman happened to be white. I can only speculate that this choice by Harvey was viewed as rejection and betrayal at its worst within his family, and that my mother was representative of all of the cunning and wickedness ascribed to those white people viewed as enemies of Black Americans. (Truth be told, Cory and I were bastard children in the reverse order of the old slave plantation south. Harvey was the figurative slave owner who came to dance with the forbidden fruit at night. There was no love or commitment he just liked to dance).

Aunt Mattie was a savior and this would be the second time that she had helped my mom and I. Remember when Harvey rescued us from that room that was unfit to live in, this is where he brought us, and mom and I lived with her our first couple of months.

I remember Aunt Mattie being very portly and looking like the attendant to Scarlet O'Hara in the movie 'Gone with the Wind'. Mom said she was all "sugar and spice and everything nice". She dotted on me and loved me like a loving Aunt does. I wish I could have been able to get to know her but she died of cancer around 1977.

This first memory is a little fuzzy but I am clear about opening the front door and discovering in the three-seasoned porch area a couple of presents and an art easel for me.

This memory lay dormant in the deep recesses of my mind until it resurfaced many years later. It would become my 'Rosebud' from the classic movie 'Citizen Cane', starring Orson Wells. The story in this semi-fictional movie is about a man who is one of the richest people in the world. At the end of his life and on his deathbed, the last word he spoke was the word Rosebud. A reporter decided to unearth the significance of this last spoken word, so he searched out and interviewed a few of Mr. Cane's intimate associates including his ex-wife. Only a few people had ever heard him say Rosebud and nobody was able to make a connection of Rosebud with a person, place or thing. In the last scene of the movie under the glow of a fire burning in a nearby fireplace in what use to be his gigantic mansion, the camera pans slowly over some of his possessions that are being gathered for removal and or destruction. In the middle of it all, inconspicuous to anyone is a children's snow sled. As the camera zooms in on the sled, the manufactures riveted nametag is seen. The name is Rosebud.

Rosebud had represented the greatest period in his life when life was simple and joyful. He had collected many of the world's treasures, had more money than a person could spend in ten lifetimes, but it paled in comparison to the joy he received when he went sledding down the hill as an innocent kid. The movie opened with him as a young boy sliding down the hill on Rosebud in childlike glee with no responsibility other than being home on time to eat. I too conjure up the same emotions when I recall sledding with Phil and Mike on pillows of freshly fallen snow from heaven. In our snowmobile suits and with dime sized snowflakes raining down on us, we were living inside a Norman Rockwell painting. Life was free, easy and peaceful. It was beautiful with a capital b. I totally can relate.

A handful of times in my twenties and thirties I thought about this first memory of mine. Why did I remember this event and not something before or immediately after like seeing my brand-new little brother which was more remarkable. I remember nothing else about the easel or the presents, including opening them up or playing with them.

Forty years later I would understand those gifts were more than just toys but were symbols of future blessings I would receive. My joy was ahead of me on a course that would increase with time, whereas Citizen Cane, who was king of the world, had only a fleeting memory that eventually flickered out when his candle of life was extinguished.

After my mother gave birth to my little brother Cory, Harvey picked her up at the hospital, then me at Mattie's house and then dropped the three of us off at the curb by the duplex we were living at. Two months earlier Harvey had told my mom that he was going to stay with her and me until Cory was born and then he was going to leave. Mom told him that he didn't have to wait. Moving fast enough so as not to get hit by the screen door, Harvey hitched up his horse and left. They had been living off and on together for three years. Four months later, Harvey who was a guidance counselor at North High School in Minneapolis, would marry a young eighteen-year-old white girl who just graduated from the same school he worked at. Was it love or lust that brought them together? My guess is lust, because four months later they were divorced. Harvey would tie the knot with at least one other woman that I know of later in life.

I mention the color of her skin because Harvey loved white women but grumbled about white people on the few occasions we would be together as adults. I hated his racist sentiments and his hypocrisy. The last time I ever saw him I had been over his house. He took out an old photo album and showed me the pictures of his conquests or (victims). I had a sickened feeling. I thought this was something only adolescents did.

After my childhood amnesia began to dissipate and the clouds of fog start lifting, I found myself in the year of 1970. I was five years old and living in a house at 1507 Oliver Ave N. How long I had been there I do not know, but soon thereafter I would find myself living at another house at 1523 Newton Ave N. A few years back when my kids were very young, I took them on a drive showing them the houses where their old dad lived. For them it was another day in the park, for me it was a time machine back to the past. The movie camera inside my head began to replay and I saw myself as well as other people. The movie showed a little boy without a father wandering and exploring, going farther than he should at his young age and putting himself in harms way. Whether it would have been true or not, I do not know, but I saw a future of hopelessness there for me. After a few seconds of my mind leaving the body, the scene began to fade and a new scene came into view being vivid and clear. It was the present and I was a husband, and a father. I had a job, lived in a nice house in a nice safe residential area and most important my two beautiful children were healthy and happy. Years later when eighteen year old Ajaa and I were passing through this same area, I jokingly tried to guilt her because of her lack of enthusiasm she had when she was three years old. She looked at me, smiled and said, "What would you expect from a three year old?"

Back in the day when my mother was born, North Minneapolis was a middle class white community with a large Jewish population. When I was born the Jewish population began their exodus toward the next ring of suburbs and a large majority settled in St. Louis Park, leaving the vacuum to be filled with people who had more melanin in their skin. I have often wondered was it because of me or were there other reasons why they moved away. Sadly, today this area is filled with much poverty and is the breeding ground of many of our states violent crimes. Because of the void created with the absence of the father, gangs have become the surrogate daddy for many young black teens.

The pendulum that once was on the side of father led families that went to church and leaned on God has swung to the other side with government becoming the caretaker and provider. From 1960 to 1995, the number of African-American children living with two married parents dropped from 75% to 33%. Also, compared to a current national average of 40%, 69% of African-American births are to unmarried mothers. Is there a connection between poverty, violence and the incompliance of God's commands found in the bible for sex and marriage, I am convinced of it.

During the time when I was five and six years of age, I remember having no restrictions from my mom that said I was not allowed past this point from our house. If she did tell me, my selective hearing tuned her out and dialed to another frequency that said 'your suggestion has been noted.' With age and maturity I have learned to master the art of listening and obeying but sometimes in the present when the 'honey do list' is being orally transmitted I experience vestigial rumblings. What this meant was I was the Captain of my ship, and I began to sail farther away from home than a little boy should go. How much of that was related to my mother's naivety about potential child harm I do not know. There was not yet a nationalized pandemonium about child predators until 1989 when the abduction of our local Minnesotan kid named Jacob Wetterling occurred.

On one of my sailing voyages (walking) down Sheridan Ave. in the middle of the afternoon by myself, a young man standing on his porch stoop told me to come up to his door. I was a little lion cub separated from his mother strolling through the jungle into the lair of a smiling and friendly cub eating hyena. With my eyes closed I am going through the visual library of memories and I see a fuzzy picture of a young man somewhere in his teens to early 20s. He brought me inside and led me down into his basement into a small room where he sodomized me. After he was done he escorted me back upstairs and ushered me outside. I did not cry, yell or run. I do not remember thinking I had been violated, or I had done anything wrong. In a proverbial sense I dusted off my sneakers and proceeded onto my initial destination where ever that was.

I never told anyone about this and only when my mother came across this in her proofread did she find out. To say she was sad was an understatement. Immediately upon reading this she called me crying. I told her I was o.k. and that at no time in my life have I ever had any anger or psychological confusion about being molested. It happened, end of story. For the next couple of weeks my mother would cry off and on blaming herself for the incident. I can understand how she would feel, as I too would be devastated if I found out one of my kids had experienced the same thing years after the fact.

As a father I did not have a long rope for my kids. I have been blessed to have such a wonderful wife/ mother who watched our kids like a hawk. There was no way she was going to let anything happen to our kids in the child predator culture we live in today. Thank God for programs like 'America's Most Wanted' that have heightened our awareness and elevated security measures for our children. In the 80s and 90s it was be careful outside your home or you might get molested, now it is equally as dangerous inside your home with the sexual pollution that is on television and the internet. It is so much more difficult to be a kid and parent in today's world than yesteryear. Times have changed for the worse in so many areas of life.

Next door to the upper duplex on Oliver Ave. where I lived with Mom and Cory was a little girl named Amber. We were the same age and became playmates. Soon the innocent play escalated to playing Doctor and I was checking more than her temperature. On three occasions as inconceivable and frightening as it may be, we engaged in horizontal wrestling. The only explanation for me remembering this and having no other memories of us doing anything else is probably because it was so wrong that it harmed my spirit and made a lasting impression. While our single mothers were doing whatever they were doing, we quietly went into the basement and placed a plastic wading pool over us, went along side her house that was shielded by a fence and bushes, and lastly my mother's bedroom closet. Only on the last occasion were we caught and this put an end to our adult like relationship until she and her family moved away not to long after. "Amber go home" was the only thing said as mother opened the door and came upon her son four years removed from wearing diapers wrestling half-naked on the floor with the little neighbor girl. Amber went home and nothing was ever said to me that day or any day thereafter that I remember. Almost forty years removed from these incidents and I look back and say "wow", I can't believe it happened.

You may ask how this could have ever happened. Some people may suggest that I was attempting early in life to break the morally insane, self professed and exaggerated claim of 10,000 by Wilt Chamberlain the famous NBA player. In actuality it is nothing more than 'monkey see, monkey do.' If a little boy and/or girl see things that they should not see like waking up at in the middle of the night and seeing their mother's boyfriend having intercourse in the living room with the lady downstairs while their mother was sleeping as I did, or accidentally surprising a babysitter and her boyfriend in the bedroom like I did. It would follow that they would attempt to copy that behavior. I share these troubling truths to remind parents to be very protective and shield their kids from all sexual stuff as it will increase the potential to destroy their child's innocence.

Not withstanding a couple of abnormal events, I did have a few moments of normalcy in my life during this time. When I was five or six years old I went up to Harvey's cabin with him and the youngest of my older half sisters. This would be the only time I ever spent time with Marguerite until I was invited to her wedding twenty-six years later in 1996.

Driving up to the cabin in Annandale began like a firecracker, and I mean that literally. On the highway driving in front of us was a car lighting firecrackers and throwing them out of their car window. Like most kids in the 70s I had my head sticking out of the window doing my best dog impersonation before the imposed Federal seat belt law was established. Marguerite who was sitting next to me in the backseat pulled me in after the first firecracker zipped by my head. After a few unflattering words were said by Harvey, the ride after that was uneventful as we rolled along listening to James Brown on the 8 track player in the car. After unpacking I went outside to do some surveying. The cabin was forty feet from the dock and water with three or four cabins on the left side and the same on the right side. To the left of the dock and about fifteen feet out was a grove of cattails and lily pads. It would in this area on the shore side that I would help Marguerite capture some frogs and where I would see and capture a regular size painted turtle. The next morning Harvey took me out on his boat and I went fishing for the first time. We caught some Sunfish and had a fish fry later that day. The weekend came and went very quickly and it was time to go back home.

With our suitcases packed and the ice chest holding our new pets, we left the quiet and solitude of the lake and headed back to the noise and congestion of the city. The ride home was quiet and after arriving home, Harvey parked by the curb and I got out to grab my stuff from the trunk including my new buddy; my turtle. Marguerite a few seconds later got out of the car and walked around to the back and asked if I wanted to trade my turtle for her frogs. I do not remember if and how much persuasion was used but I agreed to the trade. Years later I came to the realization that Harvey probably told Marguerite before we left the cabin that there was no way in H-E- double hockey sticks that she was going to bring any frogs into his house. If there was a hidden shooter involved in the JFK assassination hiding in the grassy knolls I do not know, but I am pretty sure about this conspiracy. After saying our good-byes I went into the house and was greeted by mom.

I placed the dual climate amphibious habitat module; (a.k.a Styrofoam ice chest) of frogs next to the radiator and got busy doing other things. No sooner than you can sing the first verse of 'Old MacDonald had a farm, e-i-e-i-o', was the living room, dining room and bedroom next to the living room filled with twenty something frogs doing the 'Macarena'. No problem right, just gather them up and place them back in their dual climate amphibious habitat module, wrong! That is very hard to do since mom was hanging from the chandelier. Having mastered the art of monkey see, monkey do, I too became frightened. Besides, Marguerite was the one who caught most of the slimy creatures. So after mom climbed down from the ceiling, she made a call on our1970's standard issue rotary phone for some help. The next-door neighbor guy came over and saved the night.

If questions have arisen doubting that my six-year-old existence was not as ordinary as every other average American kindergartner, than I submit the following as that proof. While being chased by someone or something, I ran into the stiletto back light assembly on a parked car puncturing a small hole next to my temple, narrowly missing poking out my eye and receiving scar #1. On another one of Captain Wade's voyages throughout his empire, I got hit by a car as I ran across busy Penn Ave.

Luckily my skin is made out of rubber and I bounce real well. I came to a rolling stop against the curb without sustaining any bruise or injury. After dusting myself off I made a change in plans and hurriedly went back home and pretended nothing happened like all little boys who get hit by cars do. (I did not tell my mom).

Lastly, I burned my hand real bad while holding burning plastic over the garbage can in our backyard and received scar #2. I was being mesmerized by the dripping, flaming plastic and after a few splashes I looked to see where it was falling. For whatever reason, I did not feel any pain as it dripped on my other hand. Because I had an instinctive sense of right and wrong (laugh) and recognized that holes in your hand were not good, I hustled into the bathroom of my house to wash away the damage before mom saw. But destiny would not have it that way. Mom saw the hand, freaked out and rushed me to the hospital where they cleaned it and bandaged it up. This was back in the day when people burned garbage in their garbage cans. Besides the above list of your normal everyday five and six year old stuff, I also walked on the wild side a few times and ate candy and chewed bubblegum.

CHAPTER 3

FrankenDad

Somewhere in my first year of grade school my mother, brother and I moved a few miles away to a low income housing project on Hwy 55 and Lyndale Ave. Mom said that the 1st grade teacher at Willard Elementary, the school I had just left had offered to pick me up, bring me to her class and then drive me home after school. I don't remember her but it would be quite interesting to meet her and find out what she saw in me that she would be so willing to do something so beyond the norm. It was here in one of the poorest neighborhoods in the city of Minneapolis at my new home in the projects (they have since been torn down) that I would have one of my richest life moments. It would be my first test of character and first noble experience. It was also my first fistfight.

It was high noon on a summer day when Sherriff Wade went over to the playground in the center of our projects to play. At the playground was a townsperson around my age playing on the slide. He was having fun while minding his own business. On the monkey bars next to the slide playing was the town bully known as Black Bart the Meanie. As Black Bart began to harass the little boy, Sherriff Wade took off his white hat to wipe his brow with a handkerchief that was saturated with cold holy water. I (Sheriff Wade) told Black Bart that this town is a simple town with simple folks who simply want to be left alone. Or, it could have been "leave him alone," I can't remember. At any rate, Black Bart jumped down from the monkey bars threw down his cigar and walked with showdown in his eyes towards me. We unbuckled our holsters and laid our lollipops and hot wheel racers on the ground. This was going to be a man fight.

After throwing a few punches we became entangled on the ground wrestling until I had him pinned. As I was sitting on top of him, there was a small crowd of people gathered around cheering and encouraging me to keep punching him. The fight ended with no one sustaining any injury that I am aware of, except my opponent may have received a bruised ego. You know you live in the jungle when people are encouraging two six year olds to fight and whop up on each other.

To my surprise, Black Bart and I wound up in the same 1st grade class together at Harrison Elementary. In class on one of our drawing projects he had painted a picture using yellow as his primary color. He said yellow was his favorite color. I was oddly fascinated with that. I thought yellow was a girl color. Later in life I went through intense color therapy and was corrected of my inaccurate pastel color gender association. This is a shout-out to all of the bullies. If you want to be a better bully, change your preference of lighter subdued colors for darker colors that behavioral scientists say will make you more aggressive; yellow doesn't work.

In the classic novel 'A Tale Of Two Cities' written by Charles Dickens, the first sentence reads, "It was the best of times and it was the worst of times". This would accurately describe the next character that would be introduced into my life. I was six and Cory was three when the two of us while sitting in the living room saw this man in our kitchen. I asked Cory if he knew who he was and he said "no". In typical big brother fashion I told Cory to ask him, since I was too afraid to ask. This was very much like the original LIFE cereal commercials in the 70s, where the two older brothers who were too afraid to try the new cereal pushed it on their laboratory rat little brother. The famous iconic one line catch phrase was born; "hey get Mikey, he will eat anything." Mom told me when I was writing this book that I had seen Claire before but that I did not remember.

The name of this mystery man standing in my kitchen was Claire Oliver and he would become my stepdad. Claire was born in New York, and sent to Alabama with his identical twin brother at the age of six to be raised by his aunt. He later moved to Minnesota sometime around 1960. Mother said she was not completely in love with him but wanted Cory and I to have a dad and was hopeful that Claire would be a loving father to her two boys. If you are familiar with the expression 'he has a monkey on his back', then to say Claire had the largest of the primates, a 350 lb Silverback gorilla strapped to his would not be an exaggeration. Six months or so into mom and Claire's marriage I recognized Claire had a drinking problem. Before their second year was in the books, I knew he was an alcoholic before I even knew what an alcoholic was. In the lunar calendar cycle, Sunday morning was usually the only period in time when he was peace filled, sober and jovial. By late afternoon and throughout the rest of the week for the next five years until their divorce, he would be intoxicated.

Looking back I realized that mom was always on edge and became more and more anxious as the seconds ticked away and the arms on the clock spun closer towards Claire's return home from work or a friend's house. Mom lived in fear and rightfully so. She told me years later that Claire beat her with his fists and open hands on a regular basis. He never did it around me. After one of his assaults on mom the police were called. I watched from the bedroom as the police kicked in our backdoor to arrest him.

Claire was a quick-tempered drunk who sometimes spilled over into the physical. The three of us walked around on eggshells when he was home. With the exception of the next story, I cannot remember the few times he hit me or gave me a spanking. When I was 12 years old. Claire hit me upside the head for something. I started crying which made him angrier. Since he did not want a scene to develop when mom would come home, which would be pretty soon, he told me to stop crying. I stopped crying but kept sniffling. He told me that when mom came home and asked about my teary face, I better tell her I had been cutting up onions. When mom arrived home she noticed right away and asked why I had been crying. Guess what I told her?

In my late 20s as I was rummaging across some papers on her table at one of my visits to her house, I saw a letter she had written laying on her desk chronicling the atrocities he had committed against her while they were married. She was going to send it to him but never did. When I came to the part where he raped her, I put the letter down and read no more. Sadly, the only time there was peace in our house and mom, Cory and I were relaxed, was when Claire was in the workhouse for domestic assault or in one of his involuntary stays at an alcoholic treatment program. Mom eventually got up enough courage and divorced him five very long years later.

Of the three of us, I was the only one who had any type of normal relationship bond with Claire. Claire enjoyed sports and because I was a pretty good athlete this bridged into a semi father/son relationship. He relished in my athletic accomplishments and partook vicariously through the praise I received from other parents. Cory, who was three years younger, a peanut in stature and who did not possess my athletic abilities, never received the special attention I received and so grew to despise Clair. Thirty some years later our abilities have been reversed and Cory is the mop and I am the floor when we get together to play sports; namely golf.

When Cory turned eighteen, he legally changed his name to our mothers' maiden name. Though we were never legally adopted by Claire, (mom said she would have never allowed it to happen), I took on his last name of Oliver. I identified myself to the only man who embraced me as a dad. His love fell very short of the bar in comparison to the love that I have given my children, but it is the only love I have ever experienced as a son in a father/son relationship. In spite of his major shortcomings as a father and husband he did on occasion do things that made a positive impression on my life. The significance and influential power of a father in the family unit cannot be underestimated. As great as mothers are, they cannot replace a father.

The "best of times" to me could be interpreted in the lone act that God used Claire like Moses to deliver the family out of the violent, impoverished inner city and lead us to a land that offered more opportunities. That land was a suburb of Minneapolis and was rightfully called New Hope. This is where I would grow up and call home until I graduated High School and went into the USAF. It was here in the second grade that the docked 'USS Starship LiL Wade' would blast off away from planet 'Innocent Child' towards the scary world of Self-Consciousness. Like most people in the world, I looked at the one or two differences in comparison to other people instead of the hundreds of similarities and focused on them. I was not a black kid in the full sense of the word because I had lighter skin with white features and I was not a white kid because I had darker skin with black features. This became obvious to me, as I was the only Oreo cookie in the vanilla wafer cookie jar after we moved from Minneapolis to Corcoran and then to New Hope. In spite of that, I was very fortunate in that I only experienced overt racism a handful of times in my life and never with the deep hatred of waking up to a cross burning in my yard. When it happened, it was some bozo throwing out the 'N' word.

Almost immediately after mom and Claire got married, the family including grandma, (mom's mom) moved forty-five minutes away to a 40-acre farm in the city of Corcoran. The country was filled with fresh air, lots of space and the pungent smell of 'Benjamin Franklins'. Country folks called manure the 'smell of money' because it increased the crop yield; city folks called it something else. We pulled onto the long dirt driveway that led to the big, old, and run down farmhouse. Unlike the city where feet separated houses and walls separated multi dwelling units, our nearest neighbor was a 1/4 of a mile away. Besides the big four-bedroom farmhouse there was a big barn that was used to house dairy cows in the lower section. It was moist, muddy and dark and since I had no desire to be snatched by the boogieman I never went in there. On the ground level section there was a couple of horse stalls and a giant hayloft filled with loose straw. If you climbed up along the wall you could stand on top of the enclosed stall areas and jump into the hay. As I am writing this I remember the smell of the stray and the itchy feel of it against my body. The barn was about a one and a half football field distance away from the house. Along each side of the worn out twenty yard wide path to the barn were very old and dilapidated buildings separated into housing for different animals, farming equipment and tools. There were no animals except mice and spiders, and all of the few tools and equipment that were left behind were now broken and rusty. In essence we were eunuch farmers who grew nothing and raised zero animals.

That would all change the day Homer came to live with us. Homer was a pig that had two different colored eyes; a blue one and a brown one. The first time I saw Homer, I almost had a heart attack. I looked over the edge of his stall and just a couple of feet away he was staring up at me. How did he know I was going to peer over and look at him? Homer had to have special powers and I knew better to ever mess with him; and I didn't. A month later Homer used all of his special powers and he pulled off a spectacular David Copperfield magic trick. He vanished into thin air. History has it that the Great Homer later resurfaced in the community and was the guest of honor at many nightly bar-b-cue dinners.

Nestled along the back of the house were about forty stacked bails of hay. One day in the middle of the summer, Claire with the help of one his friends loaded them onto a truck and took them somewhere else. That night as my little brother Cory and I were in bed sleeping, I was awakened in an Amazon jungle like way. Thousands of mosquitoes were having a picnic and I happened to be their lunch. I jumped out of bed and ran downstairs to wake up mom. With me in tow we walked upstairs and into my room. In a mothers panic she grabbed Cory and ran out of the room shutting the door behind her. The mosquitoes who had been evicted from their homes in the hay bails along side the house, had taken their revenge and had flown up to the second floor bedroom and began to kamikaze from the formation that had covered the ceiling of our 15' x 12' room. It was Pearl Harbor 1972. Except for that event, my country living was quite uneventful unless you count the time we ran out of toilet paper and I had to go outside to find and use a couple of corn shucks. Can you say 'sandpaper'?

Our family moved from the city to the country in July and four months later we would call it quits and leave the boring, quiet and odorous smell of Benjamin Franklins to return to civilization. We did not see the unwelcome sign when the mosquitoes attacked, but clearly saw it when the owner of the farm refused to fix the frozen water pump. So just like Jed Clampett of the Beverly Hillbillies, we loaded up the car and then moved to the Northwest suburb of Minneapolis to settle in the city of New Hope. Like the rural town of Corcoran we would be the first or one of the very first people of color in the community. We moved into a four-plex that was one of eight in the development off of Bass Lake Road on the other side of the street from Saint Raphael's Church. We were in the middle of your average middle-income single-family housing community.

Like us, all of the family's that lived in the four-plex's were families of little income with most if not all on some kind of economic assistance from the state. Our building was the farthest away from Bass Lake Rd and situated in the back part of the lot that bordered Thora Thorson Elementary School. There were two apartments upstairs and two on ground level. We lived on the north side of the building that allowed you to look out the kitchen window or bedroom windows at Thorson Elementary and into the wide-open schoolyard. When I introduced Claire into the story I said it like it was. He was a man who had a giant problem with alcohol and most of the time was not a very good husband or father. Out of all the few decent things that Claire would do for me in his years as my dad, this next event registered in my heart as my most endearing memory. I was never so happy in my life to have a dad and never so proud that he was that person.

It was my first day of second grade at Thorson elementary school and it was sometime in early November. Claire and mom were sitting at the kitchen table drinking coffee watching and waiting for me to come out for recess. Claire was not at work because he had just separated his left shoulder and it was in a sling. The recess bell rang and everyone went outside in the snow to play. At least that was what I thought I was going to do. Before I knew it I was surrounded by about ten boys and was squaring off to fight a boy in my class named Randy Scharpen. I laugh now when I think about it, because Randy had on one of those old 1970 corduroy jackets that would be against the law to wear today. His crime would have been classified as 2nd degree murder of the retinas.

In class before the recess bell rang, Randy who was the 'alpha dog' in second grade began feeling me out (my guess), to determine if I posed a threat to his kingship. I had a feeling trouble was lurking around the corner. Once outside Randy unleashed his profound name calling skills and called me "chocolate". How he knew that was the very worst thing you can call someone I did not know, but it made me mad and I said so. He had backed me into the corner and now it was time for my very first elementary playground fight.

Before we had an opportunity to start tangling, Claire who had been sipping coffee with mom waiting and watching for me to go outside for recess had jumped over the chain link fence and ran over to protect his son. It would not have been difficult to see me from there or from the moon if they were up there sipping coffee. The ground had a blanket of white snow and I had a 9" jet black domed afro. Stevie Wonder could have seen me. Claire sprinted toward us yelling waking up and emboldening Tracy the demure playground lady to step in and halt it before it began. He was my hero and I loved him for it.

Randy Scharpen and myself would grow up together to become friends as well as teammates and competitors in football and baseball. I would beat him out for the starting quarterback position in 8th and 9th grade and he would eventually become the starting varsity quarterback at our high school. My last year of football would be in the 9th grade. I was unwilling to accept the hard work and discipline it would take at the high school level and chose the foolish road of smoking dope. Later in life I would have the joy of watching my son Arias, an All-Conference outside linebacker play for the 3rd rated high school football team in the state at Spring Lake Park. After we graduated I would not see Randy until his 40th birthday party. Randy still looked great and still has that million-dollar smile; it was great to see him.

Me and mom playing a game.

Second grade produced my very first official best friend; Phil Nicholas. Phil was the first of my friends who would get married and have kids. After graduation he joined the Navy in 1983 and I have not seen him since. Second grade came and went and was uneventful with the exception of being chased by my next door neighbor's squirrel monkey. The monkey lost its temper, lunged at me and I jumped back landing on the metal edge of its cage gashing myself on the neck for scar #3. I did not tell my mom (again) but she saw my open wound later that night while tucking Cory and me into bed. No hospital visit this time, just a little soap, water and little love. Life sometimes deals things in pairs and twenty years later when I would take my kids to the zoo, I would have another angry primate try to hurt me.

In 3rd grade I enjoyed reading and was the class champion for the most books read. My chief competition was Art Sorenson. If he had a flatulence problem I do not remember, but that did not stop us from calling him Art the fart, pretty clever for third graders, huh? Third grade was my first year of organized football, and I played for the New Hope Vikings. Claire was the head coach and I was his star halfback; as he said.

I remember two things about the season. First, Claire had taught me to play with an aggressive attitude on defense. This entailed talking trash to the player on the offensive line who was trying to block me as well as biting any player when you were in the middle of a pile after the tackle. The preferable player to bite was the ball carrier. One time at the bottom of the pile, I made a dental imprint on the butt of a player. Every German shepherd in town came running to the field because of the high-pitched scream. I got out from under the pile of players and went back to my teams huddle. I proudly acknowledge that as of today I have thirty-seven years of butt biting sobriety under my belt.

The last of Claire's ignoble football strategies that I adopted and did happened when I was playing at Hosterman Jr. High in the eighth grade. We were playing against Sandburg Jr. High and I was the nose-guard on defense. Being lined up directly across from the center, I began telling him how I was going to hurt him. He became so afraid that he began blocking me using the Spanish "matador" technique. After hiking the ball he moved to the side offering little resistance and I would rush through his red cape and tackle the quarterback or running back. After halftime, the coach on the other team substituted "El Toro" with a center who did not speak English, was hearing impaired or was simply not afraid of me, and my backfield meetings with the quarterback and running-back came to an end.

My first year of football began with tingling excitement coursing up through my body and ended with dejection trickling down the back of my legs. Sometime at the end of the season I had asked permission to leave practice and go to the little boy's room. After the third plea, Claire gave me permission to go. Long story short... I walked the 1/8 mile to the school and right before I unsnapped my football pants, I filled my pants with mom's dinner from the night before. I went back and told Claire what had happened and that I had to go home.

I began the mile walk home seething at Claire for not letting me go earlier. As I was walking my mind began to shift to another concern. Was I going to make it home unnoticed while leaving a trail of yesterday's dinner dripping on the sidewalk? I made it back to the projects without being stopped for any sanitation disposal laws I may have been breaking and entered through the circumferential back alley avoiding any people who might be in the front. I entered the building through the common backdoor only to find mom was not home and the door was locked. I went outside in the back and saw between the buildings Phil out front playing. I called Phil and he came over. I told him what had happened and asked for some help. He ran into his house and came out with a can of Lysol disinfectant. From my waist down I had no germs.

CHAPTER 4

UFO's, Police Chases, and Car Crashes

It was an early Sunday morning around 3:30 am when Claire came into my bedroom after a full night of drinking to wake me up. He told me to get out of bed and to go look outside of the kitchen window. Groggily I got out of bed and walked into the kitchen and looked out of the window. I didn't want to get out of bed but he was insistent. I looked out of the window into the clear of night against the snow blanketed ground, and in the sky about forty yards to my left and about sixty yards in the air were three disc shaped flying saucers that were hovering in a stationary position. One of them was bright yellow and I cannot be absolute about the others but orange and red pop into my head. I locked my gaze on them for about three to four seconds and in perfect union they zipped off in a 45-degree angle towards the sky and disappeared from my sight in a second of time.

    I never understood why they appeared until later, but I have always been convinced that they purposely gave me only the minimal amount of time needed for me to register what I was seeing before zooming off. With the wonder of what I saw coursing through my veins, I stayed up the rest of the night in the living room and listened to records on our Curtis Mathis rent to own stereo system. Claire had gone to sleep so it was just me awake sprawled on the couch. I remember listening to Aretha Franklin's greatest hits album and then turning on the radio. I didn't need any confirmation from anybody about what I saw but when the person speaking on KMOJ radio station said they had seen the same thing I saw, I was pretty amazed.

    Years later while studying and growing in my Christian faith, I came across books and articles devoted to UFO'S and demons. Starting in the

3rd chapter of Genesis going through to the 20th chapter of Revelation in the bible, God says there is an invisible reality beyond are perception that is inhabited with many types of spirit beings. One of these groups is fallen angels called demons and I am 100% convinced they are the puppeteers behind the UFO phenomenon. Here is why I believe there is a demon/UFO connection. Many people who have had close encounters of a third kind, defined as communication contact with aliens have been told by the aliens (demons), that the bible is not true and/or Jesus is not God but another alien like themselves. I find it quite unreasonable for beings to travel from a distant galaxy to our small planet and tell us that Jesus is not God. Could it simply be a diabolical act of subversion cloaked in a feigned benevolent love? Why do all of the close encounters of the third and fourth kind, (fourth kind being abduction), consist only of bible defined non- believers?

In addition, these secretive and caring, inter-galactic friends have mentally molested and repeatedly tormented many of their human contacts. Lastly I offer the most obvious question. Why do these Einstein-ish, Mother Theresa like beings only reveal themselves to single tooth Sally and Joe Schmo who live in the boondocks at night, and not openly in the daytime at the State Capitol where they and their spaceship can be objectively verified? What do I know; I still think the world is flat.

While writing this book I would periodically give mom a call so she could verify the accuracy of certain events and also help fill in with some details. This next entry is something she said happened, and something I totally do not remember. Months later I would ask her about it again and she said, "I already told you. It is too painful; I do not want to talk about it again". This of the many crazy things that would happen to me in my life should have made a lasting impression, but it didn't. Was it because it was so traumatic that the mind blocked it out for my protection, or that God had so encapsulated me in his loving protection that it washed my memory bank clear? Hmmmm, makes you wonder.

Claire was drunk (what's new) and had taken me with him on his motorcycle. Mom tried to prevent him from taking me but to no avail. She called the police and told them what had happened. Mom said that four city police departments got involved. New Hope, Crystal, Brooklyn Center, and the Golden Valley police departments chased Claire in their squad cars with me on back. When he crossed the city limits into the next police jurisdiction they would be waiting for him and would take over in chasing and trying to get him to pull over. Two hours after the initial phone call I was taken from Claire and given to my mom who was waiting at her sister's house. While I don't remember that motorcycle adventure I do remember being on the back of his motorcycle another time when he had to lay it down. He gunned it down our alley street and when he applied the brake to slow down and take the corner, he recognized there was no brake. Someone who did not like Claire had maliciously cut his brake line prior to our ride. With no other safe recourse than to lay it down, we slid on the sandy gravel and went crashing into the large community garbage hopper. Claire burned his leg pretty bad against the hot exhaust pipe and had his leg skinned pretty bad from the gravel, but miraculously I received no injuries at all. Once again the God I did not know (yet) had protected me from injury or worst yet death.

During this time Claire had a beautiful metallic blue, late 60s Chevy Nova that was built for speed. He loved racing and on one occasion took me and Cory with him to watch the stock car and dragster races in Brainerd. If there ever was a James Bond secret agent man with multiple identities Claire was the man. On this occasion he told various people in security that he was part of the racing pit crew. This got us back in the Christmas tree light area where the dragsters and funny cars bleached their tires and smoked them. It was cool but too loud for me. When I would tag along with him and we were a little ways away from the house, I would ask him to let me drive the car. There was a total of about thirty times when he put me on his lap and let me steer while he did the pedals. On one occasion we went zipping around a corner to fast and I was unable to make the turn. He hit the brakes and we slid into the curb. Except for a flat tire there was no other damage. Because of these periodic lap-driving sessions, I received an honorary certificate of driving excellence (in my head), and concluded I had no need for a real drivers license. With 3 ½ years of driving under my belt, it would only be reasonable to presume that I was now ready to drive the highways at the tender age of eleven.

This next incident starts out with the same denominator of every other previous happening; Claire was not thinking clearly because of alcohol consumption. I do not remember if I asked to drive or he asked me, but I wound up sitting in the drivers seat steering and working the pedals all by myself, with Claire sitting next to me in the passenger seat. It was sometime in the winter and I was driving south on Hwy 100. I just went past the 36th Ave intersection when Claire told me to roll up my window. I told him "no I can't do it". I was fully aware of my inability to take my left hand off of the steering wheel to feel around for the window crank and drive safely. (This is my first time driving by myself on a highway, I am eleven years old, lets be reasonable dad, cut me some slack and let me drive with two hands.) He told me to roll it up again and I echoed the last thing I said, "no I can't do it". He insisted and as soon as I started to roll up the window the car started swerving. I panicked and quickly over adjusted the steering wheel left and then right and then left and then right.

I remember glancing in the rear view mirror anticipating a car running into me but thank goodness all of the cars began slowing down and kept their distance. About five seconds later, the last fishtail sent us twenty feet up the embankment before the Duluth St Exit facing the opposite way. There is no doubt that if this would have been in the middle of the summer the outcome would have been much worse, but since the ground was blanketed with a foot or more of snow I was unscathed again. Claire bumped his head on the dashboard or window causing a temporary daze and increased sobering. I had never yelled at Claire before but this time I yelled at him saying "I told you I shouldn't have rolled it up". We got out of the car, walked down the incline and walked along the highway to the service station to get a tow truck to pull it down. I am willing to bet anyone that my guardian angel has earned more medals of meritorious valor than their guardian angel.

Before my third grade school year ended, the family packed their bags and in February 1974 headed West in the old (station)-wagon out to California for a better life. We stayed with a friend of Claire's named Paul Crump in Sacramento for two months before moving and settling in San Bernardino. From Sacramento we drove south and made an uninvited stop and two day stay at one of Claire's relatives' house in Los Angeles. This relative who I believe is named Herbert Oliver, made it possible for our family to move into our two bedroom row style four-plex because of his reference for Claire.

It was here where I saw my first black widow spider, hummingbird and shepherd who periodically would bring his herd of sheep to graze on the property outside of our fenced in development. I learned how to swim, play handball, soccer and bio-intuitively strengthen my lungs to filter out the smoggiest air in the United States. Directly across from me in another row of apartments was my soon to be friend named Martin Zavala.

The elementary school I went to had a higher ratio of Hispanics than any other ethnic group. Blacks and whites were in equal percentage if my memory serves me correctly. At school I had a paper girlfriend named Cynthia. She was a beautiful ebony skinned girl who could run like the wind. Our only contact was in the form of letters using Martin as the messenger. We were to shy to actually talk to each other. During recesses and gym class it was always hand ball, tetherball or soccer which was my favorite thing to play. I enjoyed school and I never woke up not wanting to go. But if there was one thing that was not to my liking it would easily be the kid in my classroom named Ignacio V. He was the most gifted athlete I had ever seen as well as the meanest and toughest. I feared him like no other kid. One day in class we got into an argument and he karate kicked me in the face. I did nothing recognizing it was better to have a size 7 tennis shoe imprint on my face than looking up at my body from a detached head. I hope this is not true, but I would not be surprised if he was killed in a gang fight or drive by shooting latter on in life, or was sent to prison.

One day when I was tagging along with Claire in the car, we came upon a youth football team practicing. It was a traveling football team in the neighboring city of Rialto that was for fifth and sixth graders. There is a scene in the movie 'Remember the Titans' that parallels what Claire and I would do. We both got out of the car and walked up to the coach. Claire the Barnum and Bailey salesman probably said something like I was the greatest thing since sliced bread and that if they wanted to win they should add me to their roster. Coach said come back the next day and I did. In spite of being in fourth grade, I made the team as the starting nose guard, and Claire was their new assistant coach. I had a few moments where I rose to the top like cream and a couple where I sank to the bottom like a boat that had been torpedoed.

In my third or fourth game I caught a very bad case of the poultry virus called the 'chickens'. In pregame warm-up someone on my team pointed across the field and said that the Goliath of a player on the other team was their center. Since I happened to play the nose-guard position, this would place me six inches in front of this pituitary gland nightmare. In what was less than four hundredths of a second, my brain sent a signal to my central nervous system, telling it to power down and go to standby. Only because I had residual power left to move my skeletal system was I able to walk over and tell the coach that I was not feeling well and would not be able to play today. My replacement started the game and after the first defensive series came back to the sidelines saying the big guy was nothing but big. In what can only be seen as a medical mystery, the Chicken virus left as soon as it came and my central nervous system powered back up. I walked back over to the coach and told him I was feeling better. He said o.k. and I played the rest of the game.

I was never a momma's boy in the sense that we hung out and did stuff together. I was like most boys who played outside, watched Speed Racer and worked on the mathematical calculations trying to fuse Einstein's theory of relativity into Jet propulsion. When I did have alone time with a parent outside of the house, it was always with Claire and his traveling companions Mr. Strawberry Boonesfarm or Mr. Rum. Mr. Boonesfarm and Mr. Rum did not like to play catch, shoot baskets or take bike rides, but loved to play Cops & Robbers. On one of those occasions we happened to be at KMART when Mr. Rum told Claire there was a 'Blue light special' in front of the store. Claire looked and saw a guy dismount his motorcycle and park it on the sidewalk under the overhang right next to the entrance and exit doors. When the motorcycle owner went into the store, the game was on. With the help of a friend who was with him (not Mr. Rum), they loaded it in the back of his friends' truck and skedaddled away. We drove home and wheeled the 'blue light' special from KMART into our small fenced in backyard. Claire told mom that it was his friends. Mom gave him a 'yeah right' look, knowing it would be in vain to challenge him.

No California story can be complete without the normal everyday occurrence of watching a 1st grader running down the street from his father in an attempt to escape a spanking. Cory and I were at the park longer than we should have been and when we came home Claire greeted us with his pants 'holder upper'. Its Latin name is called 'Bottom-warmus-upus'. Belt is the name of its English equivalent. As I was having my backside warmed up, Cory who was scheduled next on the judicial docket realized he was late for a Passover engagement and sprinted out of the front door.

Cory's plan was quite simple. Alternately place one foot in front of the other as fast as he could while pumping his arms. If fast enough he would flee the angel of death and enter into a safe zone in the Promise Land. Neglecting to factor in his need for Moses to be there to have the Red Sea crash down on his pursuer, Pharaoh Claire caught the little descendant of Abraham and administered a thermal throbbing with the 'bottom-warmus-upus'. The late and honorable Charlie Chan eloquently sums up the last of my moral nuggets of wisdom. "He, who hides belt before play, need not run to Promise Land in May".

Our stay in California would be short and semi-sweet. Mom told Claire that she wanted a divorce and that she was going to move back with me and Cory. Somehow the totality of that never materialized and the four of us moved back to Minnesota after I completed the fourth grade in 1975.

CHAPTER 5

Trouble with a Smile

We arrived back in New Hope but in a different part of the city. Our new habitation would be a two bedroom apartment in the Oregon Estates complex off of Rockford Rd and Oregon Ave. I would attend Forest Elementary School and be in the fifth grade, this would be my fifth elementary school in my first five years; six if you count kindergarten.

On my first day of school at Forest Elementary I was tested by the resident class alpha dog in gym class. Without throwing any punches I growled, called him a "punk boy" and he put his tail between his legs and relinquished his position at the top. One of alpha dogs buddies; Donny Cooper, was there and we would later become friends. We have not seen each other often, but over the years when I would happen upon him or his brother Dan, we would all light up with a smile and greet each other with a 'punk boyyyyy'. It was like the Budweiser greeting of "What's uuuuuuuuup?", only you drag out the 'y'.

The beginning of my juvenile delinquency would have its roots here. I wish I could say that some incorrigibles corrupted me but rather it was more like 'birds of a feather flock together'. My bad boy vandalism would not truly start until 7th grade; this was just 'Norwegian street skiing', commonly called bungeying. For all of you warm climate states that don't get snow, bungeying is when you grab the rear bumper of an unsuspected vehicle and they pull you down the street over some nice fresh snow and ice.

On one occasion I was with a few of my classmates after school. We stood in front of a stop sign and waved our arms pointing to our wrist. Cars would interpret this as sweet young boys wanting to know what time it is so they can get home on time to do their homework and chores.

While they were thinking that, we would all take turns with one or two of us sneaking out of the bushes and latching on to the bumper. The front accomplices would wave and say thank you and then watch as the car went down the street giving a free, fun and illegal ride to their partners in crime. After school when the bus dropped me off, I tried to apply my new trade but the bus driver was "Smarter than a 5th grader" and told me to quit it.

In fifth grade I found out that I was a pretty good chess player. I played first board for our chess team and this matched me against the first board player for one of the state elementary powerhouses; Thora Thorson Elementary. In what can only be viewed as a monumental upset, I beat their first board. For you chess players out there, I played a double dragon defense. Though that was a big accomplishment, my biggest triumph was when my fifth grade chess coach Doug Shufeldt and I teamed up and entered a doubles tournament finishing in 1st place. The competition had many strong youth and adult players who individually were stronger than the both of us but not collectively as a team.

The following year I would transfer to Thora Thorson for my final year of elementary school. This was the same school I had gone to in second and third grade. Our chess team at Thorson was very good that year and we won the Elementary State Championship in 1976. For the first three quarters of the year I played the second board and the last quarter of the year I was the first board, but in all truthfulness the better player was Joe Longen who became one of the strongest chess players in the state. The team that came in second in the state was Abraham Lincoln Elementary. They went on to win the National elementary title. Unlike Lincoln who had saved and planned for the National event, we didn't and thus never went. Because they won the National Elementary title, it validated our team as one of the strongest chess teams in the nation. Even though we did not enter the national tournament I like to believe that we were the best elementary chess team in the United States in 1976 because we beat the champs at the state level.

Winning the team championship for the state elementary school came with a little pain. I had taught my best friend Mike Mulvey how to play chess and he became a good player; good enough to earn the last spot on our fifth man team. In round six or seven, there were a total of seven rounds; Mike had upset one of Minnesota's chess prodigy's who played for our rival Lincoln Elementary. Tim Rademacher was his name and he would become the best player in the state in the 1980s. Because of Mike's upset and our collective wins as a team, we edged Lincoln by a ½ point for the championship. Mike had a wonderful tournament and had out performed me by a ½ point to win the trophy as the first or second best sixth grader.

After getting pictures of our team in front of our school with our Championship trophy and medals we all went home. As Mike was celebrating his success with his new trophy above my head separated by the paper thin ceiling, (Mike lived above me) I was downstairs in my house crying, being consoled by mom. I was the better player; I had taught him how to play and he is the one with the trophy? It took awhile before the pain went away, but it did and I became very happy for him. On that weekend Mike got what he deserved because he optimized his ability and played like Gary Kasparov the greatest chess player of all time.

Thirty-four years later I had an itch to play again so at the age of 45 in February 2010, I entered the Minnesota State Open. I played in the second class from the bottom of five total classes and came in third. If I would have won my last game instead of drawing, I would have finished in first. At the tournament I ran into both Tim Rademacher and Joe Longen. Both of them are experts and played in the highest level bracket. The on going joke between the two of them over the past twenty years is that Joe came alongside the game that Tim and Mike were playing and stole Tim's rook making it possible for Mike to win. The truth was Tim had forgotten to press his clock after his turn. Mike realized this and did not move until after Tim had noticed many minutes later. Eventually Tim ran out of time and Mike won. All is fair in love and war, and chess. Also at this tournament I had an opportunity to reunite with my old fifth grade chess coach. It was a pleasant surprise for both of us.

Fifth grade marked the first time that I had my first literal (run) in with the law. Claire, Cory and I went to the Target store at the Crystal shopping center. I do not know if we were brought as decoys, but Claire had a want for some fishing lures and equipment and I surmise had no plans on paying. We went to the back of the store to the sporting goods department. Without any thought at all, my 'monkey see, monkey do' mimic behavior surfaced as I watched Claire stuff his person with various fishing accessories. After loading up we exited the store and nonchalantly began walking towards our car in the parking lot when to our surprise two security guards came out and told us to stop. Claire immediately yelled "run" and that is what I did. It is amazing how fast you can run when adrenaline pumps into your blood, so I took off like a rocket. I ran full blast for about 1/4 of a mile. With the security guard in chase I managed to slowly increase my distance as I ran around the building and took cover in the backyard of a house that bordered the store.

While pressed against the house I watched the security guard searching in the yard of the house next door for me. I quietly waited for him to leave and after a couple of minutes; I took a long circuitous route that took me towards the old projects that I had once lived in a few years ago. After saying hi to my old friend Phil, I began to walk the residential streets toward my apartment three miles away. Halfway home I walked into mom who was driving up and down the side streets looking for me. It was told later that Claire had actually abandoned Cory at Target as to not get bogged down in his escape.

Nobody can say the Oliver's were afraid to move, so guess what? We moved again. We moved back to the 'projects' off Bass Lake Road across from St. Raphael's church. We moved into 7204 Bass Lake Rd. apt 1 and directly above me would live the Mulvey's in apt 3. You had Miss Mulvey, Jeff who was a year older than me, Mike who was my age, and then Brian a year younger. Mike and I would become the best of friends. We would live here for the next four years and these years would produce my most treasured memories of childhood. With Mike and Phil primarily, and the other friends and neighbors in all of the other buildings, I had a sense of belonging. It felt like we were all linked together in a small village family type way. An obvious component that would give cause for this feeling was the fact that we planted roots and stayed there longer than any place we lived before.

Sixth grade was all fun. It would be my favorite year of school between 1st and 12th grade. We had multiple recesses, gym, and had no homework. When I wasn't at school I was playing with Mike, Phil, the occasional neighborhood boys and sometimes Brian and Jeff. The world was small and I was king. We rode our bikes, collected beer cans, collected football cards, played little league baseball, played chess and many other board games. We played sandlot football, cowboys and Indians and occasionally bungeed Mr. Bergstrom's garbage truck. During the summer nights, the front stoops and front yard in the middle of our horseshoe alignment of buildings was generally buzzing with activity with kids and the occasional adult getting some fresh air. On a couple of occasions, all of the kids in the village between 2nd and 7th grade played "Redlight-Greenlight" and "Freezetag". Even though it was only a few times it made a lasting impression. Sadly, those simple and innocent neighborhood group games have disappeared from Americana because kids nowadays are in the house playing video games or watching television.

I had a lot of fun in sixth grade with Phil and Mike, but it also marked the beginning of my 'grayish' feeling that I had one foot in and one foot out of the circle of belonging within the ethnic groups that I was composed of. Claire had taken Cory and me with him to Birmingham Alabama to meet some of his family and show us where he was raised. I had been absent from the black community for the past six years after we had moved from North Minneapolis. When we arrived in Birmingham I was only seeing black people and had a shock to my system. The central question of the ages, 'who am I' began to chime inside of my head. Everyone was sweet and kind to me but I had an unwarranted anxiety that they were embracing me outwardly but inwardly they were thinking that I was too white or not black enough. My mannerisms and speech were that of a white suburban kid, as well as having light colored skin.

I was wrong to think that but sadly thirty-two years later when President Obama was campaigning for president, there were a few shmucks in the leadership of the black community who said "Obama was not black enough", whatever that meant. He too is the offspring of a black father and a white mother. Though it did not apply to me back then, I somehow had detected on my inner radar that this type of attitude is alive on planet earth.

It was not until I became a Christian years later that I would have a real sense of connection to people. I understand how values, traditions, and attitudes of differing cultures form the lens that people view life through, but what I still cannot understand or feel is the allegiance people have for a specific ethnic group. How many generations removed from the emigrating country does it take before you, I, we are simple an American?

The simplicity and carefree attitude of sixth grade came and went leaving behind multiple recesses, the single classroom, and boy and girl germs.

My small, safe and familiar world of elementary would soon disappear and be swallowed by the vast and giant cosmos that contained the other small neighboring solar systems. Instead of being kings and queens of school, we would now become the peasant class ruled by the much larger and more powerful eighth and ninth graders. Goodbye childhood innocence and hello middle school blues. Ready or not, it is now time to grow up; at least physically.

CHAPTER 6

Flying Bananas

Claire's last real involvement in my life was between the summer of sixth and fall of seventh grade. He would go watch and cheer for the little league baseball team I played on and was a volunteer assistant football coach on my football team. One night during this period of time, Claire and Mr. Rum took me, Mike and Phil up to Skateland to roller-skate. I was not much of a roller-skater and this would be the last time I would go until one of my children had an elementary after school get together. While we were there Claire was wearing a Chuck Foreman Minnesota Vikings Jersey. For anyone who does not know, Chuck was one of the best running backs in the NFL at the time. Sometime during his time-out, (Claire was sent off the skate floor a couple of times by the rink attendants for going to fast) young boys would come up to him and ask him if he was Chuck Foreman. He was black, he was wearing a jersey that had Foreman on the back of it, and Claire was the same size and in good shape. Claire told them he was and began to sign autographs. Before you knew it he was surrounded by a mob of kids asking for his autograph. Eventually it became apparent that a fraud was being perpetrated. Claire Oliver and Chuck Foreman both began with the letter C and both had a total of twelve letters but that is where the similarities ended; Claire was signing his name, not Chuck's. A character and a half was he.

I had never played organized baseball before except sandlot with the neighborhood boys. Mike and his brothers Jeff and Brian had played little league baseball last year for the Red Sox and were signed up to play again. Since my best friend was playing it only made sense for me to play as well. I went to try-outs and was drafted by the Yankees. I was a pretty good player and became the teams #1 pitcher and played shortstop when

I wasn't pitching. We tied for the division title with the Red Sox but they had won the tie breaker to play in a regional tournament with other league champions from other cities. Mike had bragging rights until our team won the end of season play-off championship. I hit a bases loaded triple off of the right field wall to win the game. I have been a Yankee fan ever since.

One of the highlights of the season came at the end when Sid Hartman the famous sports columnist for the Minneapolis Star & Tribune paper took the whole team down to watch the Minnesota Twins play the California Angels. The experience was made a little nicer because we watched it from within a luxury skybox. The star of the Twins was Hall of Famer Rod Carew who was flirting with a .400 batting average. Thanks not to Mr. Carew, I hold him responsible for my sub-par batting the following years in Babe Ruth. I changed my comfortable batting stance that I employed in my first year of little league that produced an exact .400 batting average. My 'monkey see, monkey do' tried to copy Mr. Carew's batting stance and it messed my swing up. I wonder what the statute of limitations time frame is for going back and suing him for damages. The reason why Sid took the whole team down there was because his son Chad who is a local sports radio personality on KFAN was also on the team. We were introduced to some of the players, munched on some food and watched the game.

In seventh grade I played football for the Crystal traveling team sponsored by Park Construction. We called ourselves the 'wrecking crew' a name coined by Claire. We were a phenomenal team that had twenty-two guys with most of us playing both ways. All of the other city teams we played had at least twice as many players. We rolled over everyone we played and won a very hard, physical battle over an equally strong Coon Rapids team 13-12. I was the middle linebacker, wingback, kicker and punter. We were undefeated and went to the championship game to play Brooklyn Center at Brooklyn Center.

In the championship game we were leading 7-6 with one minute to go. The Red Raiders had the ball and were on the fifty-yard line. They gave the ball to the halfback who ran up the middle. I grabbed him but did not wrap him up believing the other guys who had a hand on him would bring him down. I was wrong and the running-back scampered for a game winning touchdown. It would be my Bill Buckner and Scott Norwood moment. Both professional athletes who failed on the last play of the game that gave victory to the other team. Many years later I would be working side by side with a co-worker named Jim Anfinson. As we were talking about our youth sports, I found out that dirty dog was on that Brooklyn Center team that beat us. We had a good laugh and then I tried to strangle him.

During the season assistant coach Claire and Mr. Rum fired up the football team before games and practices. The players on the team thought he was great. One day in practice Coach Claire the spontaneous unthinking man/child decided to give a visual tackling lesson to our defense. He lined up on the defensive line, busted through and tackled our star running back Billy Kaufman, slightly injuring him. Head Coach Saunders flew into a rage. From that moment on Claire's coaching involvement began to diminish. My last football memory of us together happened after a practice. Mr. Rum was driving with Claire sitting on his lap. He was chauffeuring me and some of my teammate's home. We approached a railroad crossing that had just sent its crossing gates down because a train was coming. Claire did a u-turn and raced the train on a street that ran parallel with the railroad tracks to the next crossover. For me it was just another day, for my teammates it was a ride at Disneyland.

Part of Crystal traveling football team 1977. Coach Claire/dad and me in the back.

I had not seen Claire for about a year from the time football ended when he had popped back home on a surprise visit with a person from the past around my age. He was a son of one of his friends who I had only known casually. Sometime after Claire had moved out, I began smoking pot. In our time alone, our conversation drifted to pot and I showed the kid whom I cannot remember by name my pot pipe. As if it was part of the plan, which it may have been, Claire became aware of my induction into the drug world and excitingly asked me if the two of us could get high together. I can not remember if we did, but I do remember being as disappointed as I had ever been for him. A dad would never allow their kid to do drugs. I would not have minded at all if he was the hypocrite in this situation, at least I would have had some degree of respect for him. I knew after that moment he was lost as my dad.

The next time I would see Claire as a kid would be five years later when I was a senior in high school. I happened to be driving down Plymouth Ave in North Minneapolis when I saw him. I excitingly drove into the parking lot, pulled up next to him and started staring at him waiting for him to happily jump up and down after he acknowledged me. He was so drunk he did not even know it was me. He looked at me and said, "What are you looking at"? I shook my head and drove off without saying a word. It broke my heart to see that his progressive alcoholism had impaired his senses so much that he was unable to recognize the little kid he had jumped the fence with a separated arm to save.

After I got out of the Air Force I would see Claire a couple more times. I enjoyed those few times with him. During these few visits he was an older, gentler and jovial guy with a positive and optimistic attitude. What made these few visits enjoyable was that he was sober. I was always his son and he would beam with joy every time he introduced me to his friends. Only now as I write this have I discovered that I had long ago buried under the floorboards in a locked closet in the back of my mind my sorrow over not having a real loving father when I was a kid and now as an adult. What Claire had given me I took? I hated him for all of the bad stuff he did to mom, Cory and me. I wanted mom to divorce him and I was ecstatic when he was out of our life after the divorce; but I always have had a piece of him in my heart. I cannot explain it, but the little love he gave me carved a permanent impression in my soul.

In 1998 Claire died from cancer of the liver, A couple years earlier I had driven him and his wife Cheryl down to Alabama to see his twin brother who was dying of cancer. It would be the last meaningful time

I would have with him. While down there the call of his childhood birthplace summoned him to stay and he did. A few days after Claire's death I received a phone call from someone down there. Besides notifying me of his death, they asked if I would be willing to officiate and give the eulogy at his funeral service. It was very difficult giving the eulogy in front of the thirty or so attendee's because I had never done anything like that before and I had a fear of public speaking. But my main hurt and problem with giving the eulogy was I was convinced I would never see the man who was the only dad I ever had because of his rejection of Jesus as his Lord and Savior. I read my pre-written mini sermon avoiding my sad belief of where I thought he went eternally. Since I did not lie or pretend that he went to heaven, I am sure I did not invoke much hope or smiles in any of the people in the audience as they listened to the world's worst memorial tribute ever given. After the funeral I said bye to everyone and left to drive back to Minnesota. On my way home I pulled over into a rest stop where Claire, Cheryl and I had stopped on our way down to Alabama a few years earlier. I went over to one of the trees and picked a leaf. I placed the leaf in my bible in the Book of John chapter 11. I tucked it in the seam next to the shortest verse in the bible; (John 11:35). Its two words said…"Jesus wept". I got back into my car, sat down and sobbed.

Once Claire exited the picture and his disciplinary presence was gone I became more mischievous. A few of those mischievous adventures involved Phil, Mike, and me. Periodically we would go down into me and Mike's basement to play floor hockey or goof around doing other things until my mom could no longer stand the noise coming up through the apartment floor. On this particular day we happened to be digging into and exploring through my family's items in storage when we came across a large trench coat that belonged to Claire. A flash of brilliance passed into my cerebral cortex and I shared it with Phil and Mike. They were equally as bright as me and thought the idea could be pulled off, so they agreed to help.

Across from where Mike and me lived and kitty corner to where Phil lived was an older man who was a little eccentric. The plan was to have Phil introduce his out of town cousin to him. Mike and I were going to be his cousin. So the three of us went inside his building and Mike jumped onto my shoulders. We put the trench coat on and knocked on his door. The man came to the door and Phil said hello and introduced us. What made this zany was the guy did not know who Phil was other than seeing him outside if he had ever looked out of his apartment window. I reached my brown hand out to shake his and Mike greeted him with his North Pole white face. The guy was a little confused. He saw a brown hand, a white head and a funny tapered shaped guy in a trench coat. After saying hello, we did a little small talk for a couple of minutes and then said bye. After he shut the door, Mike hopped down from my shoulders and the three of us laughed all the way home.

Not much later after our trench coat adventure, I would have another moment of genius that Moe and Curly agreed to follow. The apartment across from Mike was vacated and in our cat like prowling around we found a bb gun with a 30° bend in its barrel left behind. My idea was simple yet brilliant. Why not start a practice shooting range from the back bedroom window and target immovable objects. Curly and Moe thought I had come up with the cure for cancer and excitingly agreed to participate.

The first object we began practicing on was the windshield of a car that was parked behind an adjacent building. It had not been moved in a few weeks so we thought who would care. As I write this I shake my head in wonder realizing that the original Three Stooges had more brains than this. So not letting common sense get in the way, we continued shooting.

After fissuring the front and side car windows, I suggested to Moe and Curly that we test our newly developed marksmanship skills on the hubcaps of cars that drove by? Since neither of them voiced any arguments against, it was a silent approval. As the first test vehicle came rolling towards us at an almost stationary speed of 5 mph, I took aim and shot. Instead of hitting the hubcap I hit the driver side window. The window exploded, the car came to a screeching halt, and the driver lunged forward hitting the steering wheel sounding the horn. I thought I had killed him. Curly, Moe and I panicked and ran to our respective homes, all of us a few shades closer to a bleached white. It did not take the police long at all to identify the shooters. We had been up there all day with no attempt to conceal our actions. The end result was my mother had to pay for my stupidity.

My last Phil and Mike memory is chronologically out of order but worthy to be mentioned. The police did not come, but were almost summoned because Phil had murder in his heart as he contemplated killing me. Curl, Moe and I were in me and Mike's apartment stairwell playing foosball on a portable foosball table I received for Christmas. I had another one of those Wade Oliver half-baked thoughts and I needed a patsy. I went to get a snack to eat so I asked Phil if he wanted me to make him a tuna fish sandwich. He said yes like I knew he would; hence the nickname I referred to him sometimes as Big Phil. I went into the house and opened a can of cat food. I spread it on a piece of bread and made a sandwich. I went back into the stairwell and gave it to Phil. I watched Phil enjoying the sandwich down to the last bite. After he ate the sandwich I told him what he ate. Phil was pissed!!! Smoke came out of his ears and his tea kettle whistle head began to blow. I thought it was hysterical but he did not share my sentiments. He stormed out of the building and went home. He did not talk to me for a couple of days. Needless to say, Phil never ate anything from my house again and probably to this day does not eat tuna fish.

Phil, me and Mike, 1977.

Phil and Mike were not the only targets of my prankish joking. I was an equal opportunist, and when opportunity knocked I have always opened up the door to politely say "hello". Gary who lived upstairs next to the Mulvey's in the apartment where we would later find the BB gun sadly was a hardcore alcoholic like Claire. Not to much longer after this incident, he was found dead lying on the kitchen floor by his elementary age daughters after they returned home from school. I do not know how I got to be playing a game of checkers with Gary in his apartment, but this one and only time we played, he happened to be quite drunk. Have you ever heard of the checker move called 'flying bananas'? Gary had never heard of it either. With two sweeping moves in the middle of the game I jumped about six of his pieces going sideways, front and backwards. He asked me what the heck I was doing and said it was not in the rules. I told him it was in the rules and it was called the 'flying banana'. In his puzzled, inebriated state of mind he gave me the 'deer in the headlights' look. I said "good game" and walked out the door smiling before he came to his senses.

CHAPTER 7

My Best Friend the Plant

I attended Hosterman Jr. High School for seventh, eighth, and ninth grade and was one of a handful of kids who were black or in my singular case creamy. I was liked and got along well with most of the kids, and those I did not connect with and vice versa, we left each other alone. In a school that was 99% white one would expect that I must have dealt with periodic racism but I didn't. The only problems I had were the problems common to most male teenagers and that was learning the early disciplines of studying math, English, science and girls, but not necessarily in that order.

I played football for school in eighth and ninth grade and played basketball in seventh and eighth grade. Football had me playing quarterback on offense and middle linebacker on defense. My eighth grade season ended as quickly as the Detroit Lions become ineligible for making the play-offs; that would be at the end of preseason practice. A few days before our first game a kid in gym class punched my fist with his head, breaking my hand. In ninth grade the offensive line had only enough skill to protect me on 1 step drop passing plays. Since all of the passing plays were 3 or 5 step drops, the opposing team usually flattened me in the backfield. After the third sack in one game, coach came out and leaned over me as I was lying on the field. He asked me to tell him how many fingers I saw in his hand that he held above my face. After correctly guessing on the fourth attempt he helped me off the field. A few days later I was taken to a Chiropractor for an adjustment. In the end I would finish the season and stay out of the Chiropractor's office by throwing less and handing off to the running-back a lot more.

In basketball I was a defensive specialist. That means I was not good at dribbling or shooting. Toward the end of season #2, coach gave me the black coffee without cream talk. In other words he gave it to me straight. He told me that I needed to learn to shoot and if I did not get better don't bother coming back. Giving him the benefit of the doubt, he attempted to use a negative form of encouragement versus the positive form of 'you are a diamond in the rough, but you need to practice or don't come back and waste your and my time'. Since I did not drink coffee at the time, I spit out what he said and hung up my hardly used basketball shoes and retired. It was only after I was discharged from the US Air Force that I took up the game again, and I would play it every opportunity I had. Basketball would become my favorite sport to play and would be the sport that I would injury my knee in. It lead to a total of five knee surgeries ending with a total knee replacement.

School always began with Phil, Mike and me walking to school and hanging out in my home homeroom class until school started for most of our three years. On one of those occasions in 9th grade we were sitting in Miss Santee's class. She was a very nice teacher and we all liked her. I told her about a dream I had and asked her what she thought it meant. The dream was short and subjective as 99.9% of all dreams are. The dream went like this. A dog was in the middle of the street and Mike Mulvey was driving an eighteen wheeler barreling down the road. On the other side of the street was Phil who ran onto the road and saved the dog. Miss Santee told me that I was the dog and that Phil had rescued me from the truck that was being driven by Mike who was trying to kill me. By the end of the day I was steamed. You call yourself my friend and you want to kill me. How dare you I thought. So for the next couple of days I did not talk to him. The funny thing is Mike would become an over the road eighteen wheel truck driver which is what he has been doing for the past two decades.

In the eighth and ninth grade I had the only girlfriend I would have in all of my Jr. and Sr. high school years. Her name was Carol and she was my very first love. Carol was my age and lived in one of the four-plex units with her mom and two sisters. Like Amber in chapter 2, we soon began playing doctor minus the full-scale medical procedures. As we were moving closer in that direction boom! Out of thin air, a guy had materialized and had asked her mother to marry her just after a couple of months of dating. They got married and Carol and her two sisters disappeared. I look back and totally see God's fingerprints all over this. His love for Carol and me separated us from each other, reducing all chances of us bringing a baby into the world to be raised by parents a few years removed from elementary school.

Everyone has moments where they drive on the bumpy shoulder of the road of life. After a few of the rumblings bring you back into focus, you make the proper adjustment and steer back onto the smooth safe lane of travel in the right direction. Sometimes in life people misread their map and get off the wrong exit. In my case I did not have a map, the windshield was tinted, my headlights were broke and global navigational mapping systems were not yet available for cars. So in the summer between seventh and eighth grade I exited off freshly paved Safe Terrace Rd onto the rut filled street called Temptation Alley and kept driving until I came to Foolish Curve. After traveling a little ways I took a right at Stupid Lane and drove thru the city of Brainless Minnesota until I came to a house at the top of a hill. Everyone there was having a great time so I parked my car and got out. I saw John Belushi, Chris Farley, Jimi Hendrix and a lot of other celebrities besides the mass of regular people. One of the people offered me some marijuana and for the next ten years I sat on the hill with the rest of them singing, "give peace a chance".

It was at this time that Phil had moved on to another group of less radical friends leaving the previously mentioned incidents and saying 'sayonara' to our egg throwing at car adventures and his almost falling through the roof of Taco Bell adventure. This temporary void in the triage of amigos would soon be replaced with a new hombre. His name was Mike Barrett and for the next five years Mike B., Mike M., and I would become inseparable. The mischievous level I had with Phil in the mix was wrenched up a few hundred notches when Mike B. replaced him as one of the three stooges. I do not know who was a more corrupting influence on the other, but it was a close tie between Mike B and me.

Of the friends that I would hang out with in my youth, Mike Barrett would be the one whom I would have the greatest affinity with. Our friendship would come to an end years later as young adults. We would go our separate ways as people sometimes do in life. Mike M. and I would continue having a relationship with the both of us making the phone call to the other on their birthday. We have made it a point in the past few years to get together to play an annual round of golf. Just like when we were boys playing baseball against the side of a building and football in the front yard, I would be the teacher and he would be the student. If you run into him don't ask him about sitting in his desk watching me at the chalkboard because his memory, like his drive off the tee, veers off target.

Barrett and I had a Tom Sawyer spirit of adventure and mischief. We were very much alike in all of our good and bad ways. The only difference between us was he had a head of flaming reddish orange hair, and mine was jet black. If I was an 8 on a scale of 1-10 for willingness to take risk, Barrett was an 8.5. Whereas Mike M. would go no farther than drinking alcohol in high school, Barrett and I would foolishly try acid and smoking hashish. The truth of the matter is we both fed each other's darker side and we both were addicted to marijuana.

Mike Barrett came from a similar type home and lived a few miles away in a nicer apartment complex with his mom and stepdad. His mother married a belligerent alcoholic named Frank Barrett and Mike disliked him very much. He had so much disdain for him that on one occasion he had poured out most of the whiskey that was in his big quart bottle and peed in it. Our understanding is his dad was so hardcore that he did not even notice the difference and drank it because Mike never heard a peep from him.

Mike Mulvey's mom was a single mother who had moved her three sons from the state of Maryland to New Hope after her husband died of a heart attack in bed. Mike said he watched his dad die in front of his eyes at the age of ten.

The first memory I have with both Mikes together would be a night we had all climbed up on top of the roof of Thorson Elementary School. It was around 8:30 pm on a Friday or Saturday night well past the setting sun. We bumped into a couple of kids; we talked and decided it would be a lot of fun to climb up on top of the school to get high. We all sat in a circle underneath the stars and passed a couple of joints around. After climbing down without falling and breaking our necks, the kids we met went their way and we went ours. The game plan we came up with was to get permission from our moms to sleep over each other's house and stay out all night. Mulvey and I would sleep at Barrett's and Barrett would sleep over one of our houses. It was a go for Barrett, and me now Mulvey had to get permission. He walked up the back set of stairs to his apartment while I and Barrett waited at the bottom.

The incident played out like this. "Mom, can I sleep over Barrett's house"? Michael, why are your eyes so red"? (Agitation in Mike's voice) Mom, can I sleep over Barrett's house"? She repeated what she said and then added, "Have you been doing drugs"? (Greater agitation) Mike repeated what he said. Then one of his brothers's walked out of one of the rooms and said, "Yeah your eyes are red". (Volcano erupts) Mike then responded with what would become his woefully poor justification to disobey his mom, "you never let me do anything". Without answering their question about why are his eyes red, and without getting permission, Mike came downstairs and the three of us hung out together. Mulvey smoked dope only a few more times after this realizing it was not for him and in my opinion the third degree grilling from his mother and brothers would be intolerable.

Every teenager dreams about getting his or her license to drive and I was no exception. But like a lot of things, I did not let my lack of requirements and the laws get in the way of my wants. Sixteen was the minimum legal age to drive yet I decided as long as no one knew there would be no harm to borrow mom's car and go joyriding at night while she was asleep. The plan worked like this. Both Mike's would get permission to sleep over each other's house. After my mom went to sleep I would grab her car keys and slip out my bedroom window. Both Mikes would be in the basement waiting for me. So around 2:00 in the morning the three of us fourteen-year-old boys would bring our bag full of snacks and drive around the city of Minneapolis and surrounding suburbs. We would drive around for a couple of hours and then come back and park the car. I would sneak back into my bedroom and they would sneak into the basement.

On our second expedition we went driving and wound up on Theodore Wirth Pkwy in Minneapolis. Barrett thought it would be more interesting to see if I could drive using only my sense of hearing and smell so he covered my eyes with his hands. He was high, I was high, and this is the kind of stupid thing people who were on drugs did sometimes. I went over the curb on the parkway and stopped before going into a gulley. On the fourth and final time we were not so lucky. Everything about this time was the same; fortunately for our sakes we were not high. We kept the same modus operandi with both Mikes getting permission to sleep over each other's house and me grabbing my moms' car keys and sneaking out of my bedroom window. We had only been driving about five minutes when a police car pulled up behind us on Bass Lake RD and put his lights on. I was driving, Barrett was in the passenger seat and Mulvey was sitting between the two of us. I would learn later that I had driven through a blinking red light without stopping. I wonder if not learning the rules of driving had anything to do with that?

I continued to drive along the deserted main thoroughfare of Crystal with the police car following about twenty feet behind. I wiggled my nose like Samantha of 'Bewitched' but he did not disappear. After traveling about four blocks I realized he was not going anywhere and we were in trouble. I made a left turn on to Highway 81 and drove a block before I pulled over on the right side of the road. The police car was right behind and he had his big spot light shining on the car. I slithered over the front seat into the back seat. My initial idea was to give the police the impression that I was in the backseat and Mulvey was driving; nice friend I was, huh? Once back there it dawned on me that with his bright spotlight he had to see me slither into the backseat, so I said 'lets go'. I opened the right rear passenger door, jumped out and started running. I ran through the parking lot of a business, jumped a six-foot chain linked fence, ran between some houses and hid under a car at some motel. From my low and hidden vantage point, I saw the police running around looking for me.

After about five minutes I crawled out from under the car and began a long cloak and dagger walk home ducking in and out of cover from the periodic car that went by, I would learn later that Barrett stayed in the passenger seat and was immediately apprehended by the police. Mulvey had jumped out of the driver's door and followed me up and over the fence. He went in a slightly different direction and was spotted by another police car at the end of the street. Mulvey then dashed around the corner and ran across the highway and hid in long grass by the railroad tracks. He said that the policeman saw him run across the highway and went over to search. Besides not being able to see Mike as he walked a foot by him, he also had wax in his ears because he did not hear Mike's heart beating like a drum. As Mike was lying in the tall grass he heard one of the police say over their walkie-talkie that "the black kid runs like a deer". The police would later say that they had their guns drawn after we stopped on the highway and saw me slither into the backseat.

After taking back roads I finally arrived home. I was about to sneak into my bedroom window when the police officer told me to freeze. Barrett who was already in the backseat of the police car and I were then taken to the Crystal police station. Mulvey managed to sneak home undetected and was watching everything from behind the fence that separated our projects from the residential houses. After the police left he quietly went downstairs in the basement to hide out until the morning and then go home like nothing had happened; kind of what I was hoping to do. Later that night, his mom and my mom went downstairs and found him pretending to be asleep. Miss Mulvey then took her car thieving and police evading son to the police station. Mike has jokingly said that he was caught because two canaries began to sing. If there was a bird that sang it had reddish orange hair, because the police knew to go to Mike's house and ask his mom where he was at. Miss Mulvey said he was downstairs sleeping at Wade's, wherein the police officer said, "no he's not".

A couple years later when we were sixteen and had our licenses, the three of us, Barrett, Mulvey and I were driving around town one night in Barrett's car. Like usual Barrett and I would have some weed and the three of us would be hanging out messing around. On this weekend night we did not have any weed but we had a quart of bar whiskey I had stolen from the off-sale liquor connected to the Bungalow restaurant where I worked part time. Barrett was driving this time and we are all in that Pink Floyd dimension of 'comfortably numbness'. After driving around and polishing off most of the quart of whiskey, we found it necessary to go the bathroom. Barrett pulled into Thorson Elementary School and drove onto the grass along side the building for us to relieve ourselves. After we had relieved ourselves and got back into the car, Barrett put on his baker's hat to make a couple of doughnuts in the lawn with his car. We navigated back to the street and headed towards Bass Lake Rd. Right before the intersection we realized that we were being followed by an undercover cop car. I told Barrett that we needed to get to the convenience store right away and buy some gum.

We turned on Bass Lake Rd and went about a ¼ of a block and turned into the PDQ store. As soon as we pulled in, I opened my door and concentrated as hard as I could to walk straight without staggering into the store to buy some gum knowing that the police car was right behind and watching. Barrett followed me and did the same thing. When we came out of the store there was two police vehicles, one of them being the brown unmarked police car. I walked back over to the car chewing a couple pieces of gum looking surprised and acting like everything was normal. At the passenger side door where I had gotten out, the police officer was talking to Mulvey who was in the backseat displaying unequivocal signs of being drunk. What happens after this would have to be classified as one of the most incompetent actions a police officer in Minnesota has ever done. I say this all the while affirming my respect and admiration for all of the men and women in blue who protect and serve our communities.

Because Mulvey was clearly drunk, evidenced by his hair looking like a rooster and one of his glass lens missing; the officer had taken him out of the car and placed him in the backseat of his squad car. The reason why he looked the way he did was because we were all wrestling around in the car. Mulvey was covering Barrett's eyes while he was driving and this forced me to jump in the backseat and playfully restrain him while Barrett tag teamed from the driver's front seat. I remember Mulvey's eyeglass lens popping out and Mulvey yelling, "I lost my eye, I lost my eye".

After Mulvey was put in the squad car, Barrett and I had climbed back into his car chewing our recently purchased alcohol breath masking gum and acting like choir boys. The only thing missing was a bible on our laps and an origami church hanging from the rearview mirror. Lying on the front seat between Barrett and me was a quart of whiskey that was $3/5^{th}$'s empty. The police officer asked us who that quart of whiskey belonged to. Since Mulvey was already in the squad car and out of hearings reach, we said it belonged to Mulvey. We told him Mulvey had been drinking it and that we had none to drink. The police officer took the bottle and told us to be careful and have a good night. I will never forget what I saw next.

As Barrett and I were pulling out I looked over and saw Mulvey in the backseat with his Mohawk hairdo and face pressed against the window staring at us in a shock like drunken trance through his glass frames minus one of the glass pieces. I saw the wheels in his brain spinning and trying to process the current state of reality. If all three of us were under the legal drinking age and were drinking while driving, why am I alone in the backseat of the police cruiser and Wade and Barrett driving off? Isn't it likely that the almost empty quart of whiskey that is resting in the front seat between sixteen year old Wade and sixteen year old Barrett was also consumed by them as well? I know I shouldn't have but I laughed and laughed and laughed and every time I think of that story I burst out in laughter again.

Mike M. would have to wait a year or two but he would have the last car laugh over Barrett. On a rainy night in the fall of our senior year, the three of us were doing verse 7 from Job 1 and happened to be in the area of our school. As was the norm, two of the three occupants were high. Barrett had a desire to do some baking, so he put on his bakers hat and drove onto the practice football field at Cooper Sr. High to make some donuts with his Dodge Charger. It was raining, the field was very soggy and Barrett was ripping it up going in circles. About a minute into our vandalism the car got stuck. Mulvey and I got out and tried to push with no success. Knowing that there was no justifiable explanation to the police if they came and saw us trying to dislodge the car, we left it there.

Barrett called the police later and told them his car was stolen. The next day at school everyone was peering out of their respective class windows looking at Barrett's car parked in the middle of the field at the end of one of his donuts.

CHAPTER 8

Wasted Opportunity- The School Years

When I reminisce about my Jr. and Sr. high school years, it only brings sadness. I failed miserably as a big brother. The opportunity I had to enjoy the only brother I would ever have in my lifetime and help build him up to become the best he could be was never attempted. I give two inexcusable reasons for that. Cory was three years younger than me and very small for his age. He could not keep up with me athletically and because I was very competitive I chose to leave him at home without an invitation. On the one and only time I invited him to play baseball with my friends, and me he got injured and had to go to the emergency room at the hospital. He was playing the outfield and did everything he was suppose to do with the exception of one word. He saw the ball hit and ran up to catch it. He camped underneath it as it fell down from the sky. He had his glove extended and then boom! Instead of watching the ball <u>into</u> the glove, he watched the ball go <u>by</u> his glove. Blood started squirting because it hit him in his glasses dislodging his lens and wedging it into his eye socket. Cory had ruined one of summer's perfect days to play. Why I did not just play catch with him by myself or let him pal around with me sometimes can only be explained that I was a selfish unloving brother.

Secondly, I began to smoke dope all of the time and I didn't want to introduce him to that. What type of brother would I be if I in any way allowed my fifth grade brother to smoke dope? I wasn't altogether void of normal thinking. Besides I thought, it was o.k. for me but not for him. I was capable of managing the drugs but he would not because he lacked my great wisdom. What an idiot I was. So in essence I had divorced myself from him and robbed both of us from any brother relationship we should have had. Cory built up a justified resentment towards me and became an angry kid.

Inconspicuous to me because I was not around Cory, I was blind to his smoking of dope in the fifth grade. In seventh grade Cory was sent to a drug treatment program. Part of their rehabilitation involved having first circle family members take part in their group discussion. On one of those nights I went with mom and we sat in a circle amongst other people in the program and their family members. Somewhere in the discussion Cory angrily brought up that I was using and that I should also be in here. I was thinking that you are in here because of you not me. Keep me out of it. I fended off the few questions thrown at me by one of the counselors and other participants in the same manner skilled and corrupt politicians do. I hemmed and hawed, obfuscated and pleaded the 5th amendment. Basically I said "yeah, yeah, yeah, this is Cory's problem not mine, leave me alone, end of story." Needless to say this only added more kindling wood to Cory's fire that burned against me. I understood years later that I was partially responsible for his drug use.

I look back in life and regret my rejection of my brother and choosing to smoke dope as two of my biggest mistakes. It was not until the two of us became fathers that mending began and today we have a pretty good relationship. If there is any consolation I believe I did do one good thing for my brother. He followed my lead into the USAF directly after he had graduated high school. He parlayed his boiler room operating trade into a living in the civilian sector as a heating and air condition repair guy. Through continued post military education he advanced to the highest level of certification for boiler and heating repair. He is happily married to a wonderful lady named Teresa and I have two beautiful nieces named Vanessa and Abigail.

Besides blowing it as a brother and inhaling as a druggie (at least I admit it President Clinton), I also squandered the opportunity I had in Jr. and Sr. high to discover and develop God given athletic ability and an above average mind I had to learn with. In the very old movie classic "On the Waterfront", Marlon Brando had a famous line that said, "I could have been a contender." I have always wondered what if? What if I had not got hooked on weed? What if I would have practiced getting better in some of the sports I was good in? What if I had understood the value of education as I do now? What if I had done this or that? The bible says that we all have a finite amount of time here on earth. Time is the most valuable commodity in the world. Once it is lost it can never be replaced.

Cory and me 1980.

In the last few months before the 9th grade ended Mom, Cory and I had moved to a much nicer and bigger apartment close to the intersection of Boone Ave and Bass Lake Rd in New Hope. What topped it off was the Mulvey's would move there around nine months later into the apartment next door. Also in the last week of ninth grade I would meet another kid with a bible name that would be added into the triage of Michael, Michael and Wade to form a loose net quad group. His name was John Warren and birds of a feather flock together. His home life was a disaster in the sense that both his mother and stepdad were alcoholics. Of the four of us, John had a more difficult home life. For the next three years we would hang out smoking dope, drinking beer, gambling amongst ourselves, playing sports, and other forms of mischief. John was a loose cannon and he pissed off Barrett and Mulvey quite a bit as well as me sometimes. In spite of that we had our fun. Of the three, John would be my closest friend after we would graduate. A few years after I became a Christian, I would have the privilege of sharing and leading John to a relationship with Christ. Sadly, about five years ago we had a falling out and have not spoken or seen each other since. I hope one day we will be able to reconnect.

If a year was worth a million dollars then I lost three million plus any interest going to school in 10th -12th grade. I had no goals and my only aspiration was to make sure I didn't run out of weed. I passed through High School without learning too much of anything. I took all of the required courses, and the electives I choose I took only for the reason that they would offer the least amount of studying to pass the class. Dropping out and not finishing school never crossed my mind, but either did learning. To me it was a given that I would graduate, it was what I would do after I graduated that I wasn't sure of until my 2nd quarter in twelfth grade. I recognized that joining the USAF after graduation would be a wise decision. I would get trained in a skilled profession that would give me an opportunity and increase my chances of getting a nice job after I completed my four year stint. Also I would leave the environment at home with my friends who were on the fast track to nowhere.

In spite of my undistinguished non-pursuit of academic success, I did manage to get mostly B's and C's, with an occasional A. I would start off each year strong and then wane as the school year went along. I have seen shows like Oprah Winfrey where the invited guest was headed in the wrong direction until a teacher or some other person of influence cared enough to step in and help them see the error of their ways. I never was so lucky, but about fifteen years later I would learn how powerful that person can be when they stepped into someone's life to try and help. Vonda (my wife I have not yet introduced yet) and I were helping teach Sunday school to boys and girls in the 7-10 years of age group. The church we were going to at the time was called Family Baptist. It was in the heart of North Minneapolis which is one of the toughest crime and violence areas in Minnesota. We had a bus ministry that brought kids in from the surrounding neighborhood. Sadly, most of these kids came from very poor and broken homes. Most were raised by a single mom or grandma. We dealt with a lot of aggression and rebellion from the kids as would be expected since they lived 24/7 in a warzone environment.

One of these young boys, his name I cannot remember, was a constant problem. I had corrected him a few times before and this time I had pulled him out of the class. I was angry and couldn't understand why he kept continuing this behavior. Instead of marching him to the kitchen where he would sit until it was time to go home, I leaned down to his level and started talking to him. He shared with me that his father is in prison and has been there for a very long time. That mad me very sad but my heart took a dip lower when he told me that some kid in his neighborhood had stolen a watch he was given for his birthday present. His mom was unable to replace it.

I told him that if he would return to class and behave, I promise to buy him a watch to replace his stolen birthday present. Long story short… I went to his house and gave him the watch. To see him beam with joy was all the payment I needed. When I would see him in church he was not the problem he used to be. It was not a great act of kindness that I did. The watch only cost about $15 but to him it was worth millions. I just gave him a little compassion and this tangible action softened his heart and gave him a little nudge in the right direction. This would have been the ultimate opening for me to come alongside and mentor him and help him grow up into manhood.

What I did not do in mentoring I saw other people do for another very troubled youth in our church. This boy who I will keep nameless came from a very troubled home. He had no father and his mother had a crack cocaine problem. To compound this he was a very, very big boy in girth, which opened up the door for ridicule from his peer group. He was an angry kid, but he kept coming to church. It was only in church that he received positive attention and affirmation. His surly attitude continued for many years but there were a few people who did not give up on him. In spite of his behavior that typically pushed people away, a few remained faithful in their love and mentorship. Today he has grown up to become a great young man with a warm and very friendly personality. No one would have ever thought it back then, but he is in college studying to be in the ministry. Every time I see him he makes me smile because he is such a great guy.

My last year of public education was unforgettable because it was so forgettable. I had no special moments like Sr. Prom, sport participation or any new friendships. I entered homeroom crawling before the first bell and left school running at the last bell. My 12 year marathon ended with me crossing the finish line walking backwards. I choose the path of least resistance. My schedule mirrored the Basket Weaving 101 classes that many illiterate jocks in college take. Diamonds are created under extreme pressure; I remained a lump of coal. To describe my poor attitude, work ethic and priorities, my Industrial Arts class would paint a real good picture. Event number one happened when I snuck out of woods class to go get high. After getting high I was spotted by Vice Principal Lloyd, who knew I was not where I should be. I hustled back to class and he came in and to check up on me. I didn't have time to put any Visine in my eyes so while he was talking to me my eyes were screaming back in response "I am stoned". For whatever reason, he never called me on it. This may not be true, but I am convinced that God threw up a smoke screen causing him not to act. If I would have been suspended for drug use it would have destroyed my USAF career. As you will see later the Air Force was filled with many self induced problems but it would later serve as a stepping stone into something good for me in the future.

Event number two happened when I was standing inside of my dresser, (my project I am suppose to be building which never got finished) in one of the backrooms. Mr. Bomstad the woods teacher came around the corner and saw me packing my one hitter with marijuana. He asked me to give him what I had in my hand. I put it in my pocket and said 'No." He asked me again and I said "No" again. We stared at each other for a couple of seconds and then he left. Mr. Bomstad is one of many people that I have wronged and I am ashamed of my horrible behavior. He was a good man and a good teacher and did not deserve to be treated like that. Why he didn't push it to the next level I don't know other than the reason I gave for event number one.

My last encounter with authorities regarding marijuana would be one month after I graduated from high school. A friend named Owen and I had just picked up a bag of weed from one of his dealers. We smoked a joint and were very high. We decided that we would go to Medicine Lake and do some fishing for some Sunfish and Crappies. I was driving and we were looking around for a spot to park and fish. In our search and in my buzz I had made an illegal turn in the residential area and a police car pulled me over. I was a month away from going into the Air Force and now I was going to get arrested for driving under the influence of an illegal drug and for possession of a bag of weed that was in my front pocket.

First lady Nancy Reagan was trumpeting nationally 'Just Say No to Drugs', and in cooperation with that, the military was taking a very hard stance on drug usage. My heart was beating and my mind was racing. I pulled over and stopped. I told Owen to stay in the car and do not talk unless you are asked a question. Owen was major league stoned and his eyes were screaming bloody murder. I too was very high but sobered up in light of the circumstances. Because we had smoked some in the car, the car had an odor of marijuana. I got out of the car immediately not wanting the officer to notice the smell, and asked him what the problem was? He patted me down without feeling the bag of weed in my front pocket and put me in the backseat of his car.

While he was running my license in and asking me some questions, I was peering through the cage staring at my blood red and glossy eyes in his rear view mirror. I told him that we were not familiar with the area and we were looking for a place to fish. After the license check came back o.k. he opened my door, let me out and told me to be careful and have a good day. I got back in the car with Owen and I sat stunned for a minute. I could not believe I did not get busted. The officer didn't notice our eyes or any marijuana smell in the car as well as the bag of weed in my front pocket. I played the game Monopoly before and never had played that many get out of jail cards in one game as I had just played in the last couple of months. Was it dumb luck or something else?

I cannot say it enough that smoking dope held me back from becoming the best Wade I could have been. My mom, brother, education and everything else took a backseat to smoking dope. I was snapping my fingers, bopping my head and marching in step with the anthem of the disillusioned song called 'Teenage Wasteland'. I was fully engaged in the life of Gray. Life was joyless when I was not high and I tried desperately to numb the pain with the only thing I knew, and that was smoking dope. At my high school on a warm spring day, I was watching the varsity baseball team playing. I stood behind the fence and began talking with a girl named Karen Erickson. I would have been playing instead of watching, but I got in trouble at the one and only hockey game I ever went to for drinking alcohol. There was nothing said that was deep or profound, just one of those conversations you have with someone that became more important later on in life. She was my age and was also a senior in school. Besides being very easy on the eyes she did not do drugs or drink alcohol. In our conversation I must have been asked why I smoke pot. The only part of the conversation that I remember was me saying, "If I could get high on life some other way I would."

It was completely unfeasible for there to be any alternative in life that could possible be a healthy replacement for marijuana. Pot made me relaxed, it made me laugh, and it dulled my pain. That was the good so I thought, what I didn't realize until years later was that it also stunted my growth in life's coping skills, personal relationships with family and friends, and fulfilling my potential. In and of itself the conversation was nothing, but what it said about me was I was resigned to a hopeless position of not living life without breaking the law and using illegal and harmful drugs. For me that private conversation with Karen was not so private. God had been listening and heard my hopeless resignation. Five years later He would reveal himself to me and I would begin to experience living high on life without drugs and alcohol.

June 1983 came and I was handed my graduation diploma. The graduation ceremony was filled with more than 700 blue cap and gown graduates. My mother was very proud and those periodic anxieties she had about me not graduating were put to rest. She invited Harvey to the outside ceremony and he came with wife # 4. What do you say to your father whom you have not seen or talked to since you were around six years old? I can't remember too much of anything that was said; probably because not much was said and secondly because I was mildly high from smoking a few one hitters before the event. The day was beautiful with no clouds in the sky and eventually I would march up in turn to receive my diploma. Vice Principal Stensrud who allowed me to graduate one credit short, handed me my diploma. In 10th grade I was kicked out of my typing class and never made up the credit.

After the last name was read and they received their diploma, we were presented to the crowd as the 1983 graduating class of Robbinsdale Cooper Sr. High School. Following with tradition, everyone tossed their blue caps in the air. Everything we all had learned in the twelve years of school or had not learned would now be put to the test. Some will become doctors, policeman, and work other jobs that benefit society. Others will die in car accidents, commit suicide, have problems with the law, and struggle with drugs and alcohol. What road will Wade take?

CHAPTER 9

If Uncle Sam only Knew

Within a week after I graduated, Cory and I would go live with Harvey at his house in North Minneapolis. It was not by choice but desperation that brought this on. We were evicted from our apartment because mom could not make the rent payments. She had lost her job as the business she worked at folded. What was supposed to be a special time for a mother turned into a nightmare. She had no place to live and had to swallow what little pride she had to call the man she detested to help her out. Mom told me years later that she had to beg Harvey repeatedly to let me and Cory live with him until she was able to get back on her feet. He only agreed because my mom had called Hennepin County child welfare to cancel his $50 a month child support obligation he had to pay for Cory until he was eighteen. You heard right, it was only $50 a month. Cory and I went to his house and my mom moved into her dear friend's house with her husband. Margaret and Boris were life savers and helped my mom keep her sanity. Boris has since passed, so thank you again Margaret.

A couple of week's later mom moved into an upstairs duplex behind Margaret and Boris on 13th Ave NE, in Minneapolis. She would call that home for the next two years. I stayed with Harvey for a couple of weeks and as soon as my mom got her place I left. I do not remember any one particular incident but our water and oil relationship was not blending to good. On top of that I had enough of him talking bad about my mother. I left and would never see him or talk to him again until thirteen years later when my soon to be second wife Vonda encouraged me to send him an olive branch of reconciliation; an invitation to our wedding. Cory continued to stay there but not to long after I left for the USAF, he too moved back home to live with mom. My two months of summer freedom came and went very fast and it was now time for me to leave the nest and learn to fly.

My first day of active duty in the USAF was August 8, 1983. I joined the USAF only with a guarantee that my job would be a Precision Measurement Equipment Laboratory technician. It was the premier electronic tech occupation in the USAF. I worked in a controlled climate laboratory where I learned to calibrate and repair down to the component level many types of electronic, current and resistance measurement devices. I must have had one eye open in math class because I scored high enough on the math part of the entrance exam to qualify for this job. But before I share the story about my military adventure of soaring in the wild blue yonder of the Air Force I will go back in time to my first job and move forward from there.

I was eleven years old when I attained my first job as an 'information logistics disseminator'. Most people know it by its less glamorous name of 'paperboy'. Mark Hanson was his name and he sat a desk in front of me in Mrs. Berger's' fifth grade class at Forest Elementary in 1975-76. Every day Mark came to class with all kinds of goodies for himself. He would unload and hide his treats in his desk and munch on them when Mrs. Berger wasn't looking. After a few months of wiping drool from my chin, I decided to follow in his footsteps. So I made the phone call and received an evening and Sunday morning route in my neighborhood. For the evening route I pedaled the streets making throws on the move. I broke no windows nor had any papers land on the roof. On Sunday's I pushed the yellow metal paper cart. On those Sunday mornings when I had extra papers, I sometimes stood on the corner of 42nd Ave and Winnetka selling them off at ½ price to passing motorists. The job lasted for about six months.

Two years later I once again became an I.L.D on the other side of New Hope. After a couple of months I called it quits. The main reason I quit was part of the job required me to go door to door and collect money from the past month's paper delivery. If I did not collect I did not get paid. I had an apartment route and collecting from some of those bums was quite the chore. For every two people who answered the door and said they did not have the money right now, there was one person who while turning the volume down on the television, told everyone to hush and be quiet so the paperboy would leave. Sometimes they tiptoed over to the peephole to stare at me staring at them.

About a year and a half after mom and Claire's divorce, Claire popped over unannounced. Mom told me he had done this a few other times looking for a place to crash or borrow a few dollars from her. I was in the parking lot on my bike when I saw him. I asked him what he was doing here. In hindsight, this was not a very respectful and loving thing to say. That set him off and his alcohol, saturated blood began to boil. He began to run at me telling me do not come back here until I found a job. I pedaled my bike as fast as I could to escape from him. Stewing with anger I pedaled down Bass Lake Rd not knowing where I was going or what I was going to do. By the time I cooled off I found myself a couple miles away in the neighborhood of the Panokoeken pancake restaurant on Hwy 81 in Crystal. I went in and applied for a dishwasher position. I was hired on the spot. This was in the summer before the start of eighth grade and this was job number three.

My stay of employment was short only lasting about five weeks. One evening after school I went home, grabbed my bike and pedaled to work. An hour earlier I had hurt my hand in football practice. When I got to work I walked into the kitchen area and saw piles of dishes waiting for me to be washed. I looked at the dishes and then at my throbbing hand. I told the manager that I could not work that night. He said I had to stay. I told him I was not going to. He said if I leave I would be fired. I walked out the door, got on my bike and left. As I was rolling down the retail and fast food district towards home, I saw a help wanted sign at Arthur Treacher Fish & Chips. I went in, filled out a job application and got hired on the spot. I only worked there as a fry cook for about three weeks before they fired me for being underage. I had somehow put the wrong year of my birth on the application making me two years older than I was; go figure. That was Job number four.

About a year later I would find my fifth job up the street on Bass Lake road at Kentucky Fried Chicken. I was hired as a research developer to improve the secret recipe of the Colonel. Most of the time they just had me frying chicken. Those few weeks at Arthur Treacher's Fish & Chips really paid off. If America wants to find the next great oil deposit they need not look far. Wring out the chicken at KFC and you would have enough to fill your gas tank. I told my self I would never eat their chicken after working there, but I occasionally have a taste for some grease.

Job number six would be on what street? You guessed right. A few months after working at KFC, I applied for and got hired as a busboy at the Bungalow Restaurant on Bass Lake Rd and Hwy 81. It was a fine dining restaurant with a piano and mood lighting. They had an open bar, off sale liquor store and a motel. The owners name was Elmer Hartwig and he was in his late 70s or 80s, but looked like he was in his 90's. I liked Elmer and he was quite good to me. Elmer would make the periodic stroll through the dining area and bar to say hi to the regulars. When he wasn't drinking, that would be when he was sleeping, he had a strong like for cards and an even stronger like for the hostess who worked there. She was about forty-five years his junior and they had a thing going on. Elmer was Captain Stuebing and he was rocking the Love Boat.

There was quite a cast of characters that worked there. You had Frank the gregarious alcoholic bartender. There was Curtis the overweight chef who had a scowl on his face most of the time. Doing the dishes and sweating his butt off in the kitchen with Curtis was dishwasher Dan. The waitresses were Spider, named for her long legs, Karen, Jean, Mary Jo, and a few others whose names slip my mind. They all were very nice to me and at the end of each night they gave the two or three on duty busboys a cut of their tips. I made pretty good money for a part time job in High School. I worked at the Bungalow Restaurant for two years.

In the summer between my junior and senior year I applied for a busboy position at the newly opened T Wrights restaurant in Brooklyn Center. There are three things that I remember about working there. I think her name was Joy and she was the most beautiful girl I had ever laid eyes on. I was told by one of the other busboys that she liked me and that I should go ask her out. Most guys would have taken that as a sure sign to approach her but I was too intimidated by her beauty. I felt like Shrek who loved the beautiful princess Fiona.

The second thing of memory is I only worked there for about four weeks; this would be a direct result of the third thing I remember. Whether it was me or the other busboy named Jay I do not remember, but one of us had the grand idea of stealing a case of beer from the cooler at the end of our night shift. We stashed it in his car and were going to drink it later. Later that night almost immediately after I got home he called me and said they knew we had stolen it. He returned it the next day and we both were fired.

The last job I would have before I went into the USAF would be in my senior year of school. About a month into the school year I moved into an apartment across the street from my apartment. It was the same apartment complex that John Warren lived at. I moved in as a live in attendant to a man named Morgan. Morgan was around 15 years my senior, had MS, and was confined to a wheelchair. I had already known Morgan for a few months. John, Morgan, Gus who was a quadriplegic and I played poker a couple of times. We got along great. We laughed, played cards, drank beer and smoked weed. Morgan's attendant had moved on to something else and he needed another person to replace him. The pay was $1200.00 per month and he did not have to ask me more than once. Morgan was a healthy normal man until a few years back when he came down with MS. The MS had robbed him of his independence. He could no longer walk and now required someone to lift him in and out of bed as well as into or out of his wheelchair. Once I helped drying him off from his shower and helped him get dressed he would be on his own while I was at school. To my shame I acknowledge my stay of employment only lasted two weeks.

All was well until I got mad at Morgan one early morning when he came home from hanging out with his friends in the building. I told Morgan that I needed my sleep for school and that if he came in late again he would have to sleep in his wheelchair because I was not going to get out of my bed and put him into his. Needless to say that was not received to well. His experiment to hire a seventeen year old that brought youthful exuberance into his life was not going to work. I moved back home across the street and he hired a more qualified and mature person to help. Around ten years later I was watching the local news and I saw Morgan on television. He was leading a peaceful demonstration at the state capitol for increased awareness and support for people with disabilities. I found out through the grapevine that he had become a Christian and that God had turned his life around. I made an attempt to contact Morgan and apologize for what I had done years ago in his service, but was unable to get a hold of him. A few years later, Morgan died of his disease.

August 8th came very fast and my day for leaving was upon me. Mom drove me to downtown Minneapolis around 7:00 a.m. and dropped me off at the building for induction for the new military recruits. It had a surreal feeling. She pulled up to the curb and parked. We hugged and told each other we loved the other. I opened the door and walked up the twenty steps to the front door. At the top of the steps I turned around and waved. My mom said it was the saddest moment of her life until she would repeat it three years later when she would have a déjà vu moment with Cory. She would repeat the exact same thing with Cory and he would walk to the top of the stairs stop, turn around and wave just like I did. We both went through the door into a parallel universe called the US military and into another world called adulthood.

At the processing headquarters I and the other recruits did a battery of physical tests and paper work. A funny moment happened when all of the guys in my group were told to strip down to our underwear. We were going to have the famous cough while the doctor grabs your baby maker test. One of the guys stood in his pants. What made this more amusing to me was I knew this guy. We were in the same fifth grade at Forest Elementary. What kind of guy doesn't wear underwear? Well at least you have to give him a little credit for not wearing panties. We were told that sometime before us a guy was wearing panties. Not the kind of first impression you want revealed to start off your military career.

After the battery of tests and paperwork was completed, they bused our group to the Minneapolis/St Paul airport to fly to basic training. I came into the world a perfect little boy and after I took my first breath of air, each day thereafter I became less and less perfect. I liken my Air Force career to that. Less than twelve hours into the military I would be engaged in interstate tongue wrestling from Minnesota to Texas. She was going to basic like I was and we happened to be sitting together. My recruiter never told me that the trip to basic was that fun. As soon as we landed the fun stopped and 1,177 days later it would end for good.

We arrived at Lackland AFB, Texas in the early morning hours after midnight. Divisions were made between all of the recruits that were flown and bused in from all over the country and I was assigned to squadron 3706. For the average person who may not know, each unit in basic training is led by two drill instructors. They are commissioned with the job of making everyone battle ready through a much regimented schedule of various drills, exercises, schooling and chores. To sift out the weak and break down the proud in spirit, they employ a lot of in your face yelling. If it was because we arrived late, I do not know, but they spared us the drill sergeant routine until our next day.

After basic training I heard a story about a couple of drill sergeants that went a little too far and caused quite a stir. I thought it was funny and worthwhile to mention. A new group arrived and after getting off of the bus they were told to get into four lines. A drill instructor barked out orders and told the new recruits that they were not home with their momma's anymore. He told one of the recruits to do something and this recruit said 'no'. They began to argue and the drill instructor took out his gun and shot the recruit. Every one of the new recruits freaked out and took off scattering in every direction. What the recruits did not know was that the person who was shot was actually a drill instructor posing as a recruit; and it was with a blank, not a real bullet. After rounding everyone up and giving them an opportunity to change their underwear the group went on to complete their six week commitment with two new drill instructors.

I and all of the other new recruits hit the bed around 2:00 A.M. and slept in late till about 9:00 am. From there we spent the day marching around to various processing points including receiving our beautiful pickle suits. The military fatigues were a kosher dill pickle green, thus the name. If wearing a cookie cutter, non-tailored canvas outfit was not enough for humbling; the military thought removing all of your hair on top of your head would finish the job. They shaved all of it off and I hated it. After my first buzz cut at basic training I realized how much of my self-esteem was related to my hair now laying on the floor. The thousand little sons were crying for their daddy who in turn was crying for them. My soft jet-black afro made me look better than being bald and there was never a need to answer the question was I Puerto Rican or Mexican. After the mental rape and kidnapping of my children I transitioned into the world of baldness with the rest of my squadron.

About a week into basic training I was promoted if you would call that to squad leader. There were four squads and about fifteen men in each squad. Whether I was leadership material, or I had given the impression that I was leadership material, I do not know. Being squad leader had its perks. On one occasion my squad was given the duty to go over to the NCO club to clean it. I marched my squad over and assigned them to various clean up tasks. My luck would have it that the DJ was not there and so I filled in. There was really no one there dancing but Wade Sir-mix-a lot was spinning the albums. While all of my squad members were working in the kitchen, mopping, sweeping and cleaning I was at the turntable in an elevated glass enclosed cage next to the dance floor having a blast.

Another fortunate duty assignment I received was in my opinion the best assignment in the whole unit. I was the cleaning supply monitor. That meant I was in charge of the cleaning equipment and supplies. Every Saturday morning our unit of sixty people had to clean our bay dormitory. My job stationed me in the supply room handing out all of the cleaning equipment and sitting there until they returned it. It was a hard job of sitting and waiting, but someone had to make sure the brushes and scrubbers that were used to clean the floors and toilets came back clean.

Unless it has changed the Air Force basic training conditioning of all of the armed services is the least physically demanding. We woke up early in the morning to the bugle morning call. We hustled out of bed got in uniform and hustled downstairs. If you didn't hustle and were late you experienced the wrath from one of the drill sergeants. Within a few days everyone had developed Olympic "get out of bed, put sneakers on and run downstairs to formation" speed. After finishing our Girl Scout exercises we went to breakfast. The rest of the day was filled with marching to and fro to various classes, training sessions and drills, separated by lunch and dinner. I was very privileged to be selected as a squad leader and cleaning supply monitor. Life was pretty rosy but on that rose I had one thorn.

In the barracks there was a very loud midnight airfield that jet fighters and bombers took off from and landed. The name of the runway was called Winkelbleck and he slept two cots away. One night I had enough of it so I got out of bed and crawled under his cot. While he was snoring I reached out from under his bed and hit him on the chest with my fist. I heard him lung up and I can only assume he looked around in a fog trying to gain his senses as to what just happened. He went back to snoring and I hit him again. Same thing happened only this time he rolled over on his side. After a few minutes I crawled from under his cot and went to mine. The planes had been grounded that night and victory was mine.

The six-week basic training course came and went in about twelve weeks (so it felt) and it was finally time to graduate; but not all of us would be leaving the same day.

Most of us had to be at our Technical schools right away and others not so soon. One of the guys in our platoon had to wait a couple of days before he was bused to the airport to fly to his Technical school. I heard later that when he was on the bus leaving the base, he had flipped off one of the drill instructors. The drill instructor chased the bus down and pulled him off the bus. He wound up having to do basic training all over again. I am willing to bet that when he left the second time he was waving bye, blowing kisses and telling everyone how much he loved them.

CHAPTER 10

Colonel Makes a Promise

The technical school I went for training was at Lowry AFB, Colorado. I arrived in the middle of September and this would be my new home for the next six months. It would have been three months longer but the last part of the school was self pace and I hurried to complete it so I could leave early. I would not know how important that decision would be until I left. If I would have stayed two more weeks I would have been dishonorably discharged out of the Air Force. The building I lived in was a giant dormitory. It was a nice facility that was clean and well taken care of. Unlike 95% of all of the men and women who were living there I had my own room. I was on the first floor in a wing in the back. In order for me to keep this solo living arrangement I had volunteered for the assistant Bay Chief position which had the responsibility of making sure our corridor floor was cleaned, buffed and waxed once a week. Because the bay chief did most of the work by assigning the few people who lived in our bay, I had very little work or worry. Only one or two times when I was there did I ever have to get out the buffer and clean the floor.

Tech school was college in a pickle suit with the periodic salute to your officer that went by. It was not that far from our dormitory so it would only take a few minutes to march over there. Once there, everyone would proceed to their respective class that was determined by the group you started with when you arrived on base. The course was arranged in blocks. There were 13 blocks and each block was an introductory course related to electronics. At the end of each block there was a test. If you passed the test you moved on, if you failed more than once you were 'rocked out' as it were called and were given another job or your walking papers from the military. One of my classmates 'rocked out' early on and became a bus driver on base.

There were approximately twenty people in my class which included two men from Greece. One was an officer and the other man was a high ranking non-commissioned officer. Everything was going smoothly in school until sometime in the neighborhood of the 4th block. In our classroom it was set up with rectangular tables that included seating for four students. During this block I was assigned to sit next to the Greek non commissioned officer. We were working on a project and out of no where he put his arm over the back of my chair and whispered in my ear that he wanted to do a sexual act on me. I went into shock. Time had stopped and my cerebral cortex disengaged from my tongue and muscular skeletal system. The only thing working was my heart that was pumping faster and my eyes that were looking but not seeing. After a seemingly eternal few seconds, the 6 lb mass of muscle inside my skull started to slowly recover and send signals to my chest telling it to lean forward towards the table to escape his arm draped over my chair.

Still unable to think and move, I peered into 'no where land'. Not sure how many seconds went by; the bell rang signifying a break time. This was not 1992 when Bill Clinton passed the "don't ask and don't tell" homosexual law that overturned the nations two hundred year policy that disallowed homosexuals to serve in the military. As soon as the bell rang I told a friend in another class what had happened. He told me that the guy had also made an inappropriate advance towards him earlier and that we should inform one of the military administrators. So we went downstairs and talked with someone who then called a MP (military police) to file a report. After telling them what had happened they questioned the Greek non-commissioned officer who vehemently denied it. I do not know what happened to him but he was removed from my class and I never saw him again.

There is no doubt that I was not use to the discipline and structure that the military demanded as well as the 24 hour presence of the military. I always felt like I was at work even in the solitude of my dorm room. Because I had a rebel spirit I also had a difficult time with the stripping away of individuality the military tried to do. I understand their mission to make E PLURIBUS UNO; out of many one, and to mold individuals into a ready prepared group capable of defending the country on notice. There were regulations for everything and a lot of my individual freedoms that I took for granted before I enlisted were now gone. We were in the

Cold War with the Russians and yet I felt I was living in communism like the Russians, the very system our democracy opposed. My mindset was to endure the next four years, get my education and hands on experience in the electronic field, and then get out and find a job in the civilian sector. I had two problems; one that I was gray and two that I did not know I was gray. Years after I was discharged from the USAF and became a Christian, I made a decision to never stand up in church to be applauded and thanked for my military service. Because I had a very selfish, immature and unpatriotic attitude it would be hypocrisy for me to masquerade as a veteran worthy of thanks. This is something I continue to this day.

The highlight for me while I was there at tech school was the periodic letter I would receive. Most of the letters were from mom with a few of the letters coming from Barrett, Mulvey and John. I was happily surprised to find out that they knew the alphabet and could string letters together to form words. Eventually they would get rolling in their lives and the letters would come to a halt.

A few months after I arrived, I met a guy who lived directly opposite from me across the hall. He had his own room like me and was part of a four person group that was being trained in a specialized electronics field I cannot remember. Do you remember Toucan Sam the mascot for the cereal FROOT LOOPS? Somewhere in our conversation I had sniffed out that he was a dope smoker and to my surprise he had a ¼ lb bag of weed stashed up in his ceiling. My abstinence of smoking weed came to an end. I remember going out at night and smoking it outside afraid of doing it in my room for fear of the smell. I felt so good until I had to go back to the dorms and walk through the commons area back to my dorm room. I walked as fast as I could without talking to anyone because I was very paranoid. Even though I put Visine in my eyes they were still glossy suggesting that I had just waxed them with furniture polish or had smoked some dope.

I would have smoked every day but the fear of being called in to do a random urine test for drugs scared me enough to do it only a few more times in the six months I was there. I gambled that the three or four times that I did it in tech school they would not surprise me with a call to go pee. It was a stupid risk I took, but when you are living in the Gray, you do stupid things.

Christmas vacation would come and I went home to see my mom, brother and friends. I went home with a pocket full of money and was all set to party for the next couple of weeks. The number one thing on my mind was calling my local dealer and buying a big bag of weed and that is what I did. From there it was rolling with the boys, smoking, drinking and trying to not get caught by the police. Like usual I spent very little time with my mom and brother. When it was time to head back to tech school, I caught a ride with a school friend named Scott Hansen. He was a freshman at one of the colleges in Colorado so it was not out of his way to give me a ride. We listened to music, talked and drank Schnapps while we were riding. When we approached Colorado Scott had me drive for a little bit so he could take a nap. Since I had never driven a stick shift before, I would wake him up when I needed him to shift gears. This experience would give me a false sense of accomplishment which would get me in trouble when I arrived at my first duty assignment after I graduated tech school.

I got back to tech school in one piece and began to study so I would be able to shave off three months from the normal 9 months and graduate early. I didn't particularly like it there so I wanted to leave as soon as possible. I do not remember how many infractions I had on my rap sheet, but the dorm Sergeant moved me up the chain of command to stand before the full bird Colonel in charge of the dorm. I had a meeting with the Colonel in his office and he told me if I get in trouble one more time that he was going to kick me out of the military. I was scared. How would I be able to stay clean?

About a week or so after the meeting with the Colonel I was assigned to CQ duty. This stood for Charge of Quarters and I and another guy who happened to be from Minnesota manned the front desk monitoring the security of the building. We had the early morning shift that started I believe around 10:00 pm. It was nothing to difficult, we sat at the front desk and made sure no unauthorized people would come in. If there were phone calls we would answer the phone, other than that it was just sit around, talk and do the occasional patrol. The time went by a little faster because I had been drinking before I started and then drank a few more beers in the middle of the shift.

Somewhere in the middle of the night around 2:00 am after everyone was back and it was quiet, I went into the dorm Sergeants' office to look for my file. I could do this because I had the keys to the bldg. I didn't find it so I went into the Colonel's office. Again I could do this because I had the keys to the place. I found the file cabinet that housed the personal files of everyone in the dorm. I went to the O's and found Oliver. I took all of my discipline out and stuffed it down my pants. I put the file back, closed the file cabinet and walked out of his office as if everything was normal. I walked back to my room and pulled the papers out of my pants. I took out some matches, lit all of the papers on fire over the toilet bowl, dropped them in and flushed them. After watching and making sure all of the blackened shards of paper disappeared, I left and walked back to the CQ desk and finished my shift.

A few weeks later I was told to report to the Colonels office because I had got into some kind of trouble. He looked at me and said he couldn't figure it out but my discipline file filled with my past offenses had been lost. He was going to kick me out but had to start over from square one. He was mad. That would be the last time I would ever speak with him again. I had managed to stay out of trouble from that day until the day I would graduate. Putting it in another way, I didn't get caught; like the time I was marching in formation with about forty people to the gym for our weekly morning exercise. I was lined up in the back of formation and jumped out and ducked into a patch of pine trees. Everyone continued to march and when they were out of range I went back to my dorm room and went back to sleep. It was only by the grace of God that I didn't receive my just due penalty for the hundreds of things I did that should have resulted in jail, injury or death. Thank you God for your patient endurance and mercy you gave me.

This next story is what you may call luck and what I will again call divine intervention. I had befriended a guy my age with less common sense than I had. He moved into my bay that happened to be the quietest and only bay that was not at full occupancy. In other words he would eventually put our bay on the radar. We hung out a few times together but then I pulled away from him because he was loud and careless. He was smoking weed quite often and was storing it in his dorm room locker. I completed my last block and finally had graduated. Before I left I told a few guys to watch out and steer clear of this guy because he is going to get busted and anyone associated with him will go down in fire as well.

About six weeks later I received a letter at my first duty assignment telling me that a week after I had left, the military police went into his dorm room and requested him to open up his locker. He refused so they got bolt cutters out and cut his lock. They found his pot. This began a dorm sweep and massive urine testing that kicked him and a bunch of people I knew out of the military for drug use. A couple of the guys were people who were weeks and days away from graduating. I believe they were given a dishonorable discharge, and to think I was seven days removed from that. God had a plan for me and it required me to move on to my first duty assignment at Loring AFB, Maine.

About three months into tech school I and my classmates had filled out a list of preferences where we would like to be sent for our duty stations. This was called a "dream sheet." My first choice was Hawaii, followed by places in California and then Florida. Do you see a pattern? Somewhere in block 8 or 9, I got my assignment. After looking on the map I literally started to cry. I was assigned to Loring AFB in the upper part of Maine. This was the complete opposite of where I wanted to go. I was banished to the cold wastelands of the farthest northern point in the continental United States of America to languish in the frozen tundra. Eventually the tears dried up and I accepted my fate. I was chauffeured to the airport in Denver by a couple of my classmates. For a going away present one of them pulled out a joint and we smoked it. I was dressed in my military blues and was higher than a kite; definitely not a good representative of the USAF. I said bye to my friends, checked my bags, boarded the plane and flew home to Minneapolis. It felt great to be back home. Sadly, after the bags were unpacked a few hours later I would be running with the gang drinking and smoking, abandoning my mother, the one person who truly loved me.

CHAPTER 11

Nine Lives Minus Eight

The time came and went pretty quick and I was on a plane headed to Boston Massachusetts. From Boston I caught a transfer flight on one of those small planes that you can almost touch both sides of the inside windows at once. I was being bounced around in the turbulence and I didn't know if I was going to make it there alive.

I arrived at the Bangor Maine airport around 9:00 pm. The airport was very small and I knew immediately that I had arrived in the boondocks. I was picked up by Jim and Todd who would be my electronic technician colleagues at work and neighbors in the dorm. As we were driving to the base, Jim told me not to blink because if I blink I will miss the big town that has the movie theatre and few places to eat. I kept my eyes open and watched the town go by in a matter of seconds. If I wasn't depressed when I landed at the airport, I was surely depressed now. We arrived at the base without seeing or running into any caribou, deer, bears or abominable snowmen galloping across the road. Jim and Todd helped me carry my stuff up into my new barracks that had about twenty-eight rooms on two floors. The days of having my own room were over. My new roommate would be a guy they called the 'candy man'. He was dating some girl in high school around sixteen or seventeen. It was lucky for the both of us that we worked different shifts and didn't see each other that much, because we were night and day different.

The next morning I was driven up to my new work home. It was a temperature controlled, dust free building on the edge of the base that had a small maintenance building attached to it. I went in and I introduced myself to my new boss and co-workers. After the introductions and tour of the laboratory, Todd asked me if I would like to borrow his car to run around base and go to the necessary places to complete my new location in-processing. I said that would be great and he handed me the keys. I went out to the parking lot and got in his small gas efficient car that happened to be a stick shift. Most people would have climbed back out of the car, shut the door and walked back in and said, thanks but I have not learned how to drive a stick yet. Would it be possible for someone to give me a lift? Well Wade was not like most people. When you mix over-confidence and your head up your butt you get excitement to say the least. It would be a few years down the road until God would perform surgery on me to resituate my head. The name of the surgery was called a 'Cranium Anal extraction.' It is amazing how much better you can see and think, and the quality of air is better.

It took a few attempts but I finally put it in reverse without the car jerking and dying on me. I put it in 1st gear and started driving around the building. I was jerking about and I came to a stop in front of the door of the small maintenance shop. The guy who worked there came out and was watching me jerking around in Todd's car. I asked him a question about how to drive the stick and he gave me an answer. I put it in gear and slowly left the parking lot and drove around the base. I will say that when I returned later on that day I was a pretty decent driver. After filling out all of the necessary paperwork at the base headquarters I drove back to the lab. When I arrived back everyone was looking at me. The maintenance guy next door had run into the lab like Paul Revere and told them what he saw. 'Some young brainless kid had stolen Todd's car not knowing how to drive a clutch.' Todd I am sure did not think I was coming back with his car in one piece. Needless to say my first impression was not the first impression you want to give your new boss and co-workers, but still better than wearing panties.

Besides Todd and Jim, some of the other guys I worked with were Ron, Jeff, Terry, Rocky, Rex, Bob, Paul, Bill, John and one or two other guys. I was the youngest there and the youngest ever in the history of the lab. That would change a couple of months later when another guy my age arrived, name Don. All were married with the exception of Todd, Rex, Don and Jim. Ron who was from Jamaica was separated from his wife and living next door to me. We became pretty good friends and it goes without saying that he would introduce me to reggae music.

Electronic Tech. Loring AFB, Maine 1984.

One of the adventures I had with Ron entailed driving his car down to New York while he drove a rented U-Haul. The drive through upper New York State was picturesque and serene aided by the sweet sounding rhythm of a Lionel Ritchie cassette I had on. That soon changed once we got to the city. Our course took us on the highway through the Bronx and it shocked me to say the least. There were miles of what looked like bombed out giant apartment buildings. It looked like something in Beirut Lebanon. As we kept driving, I saw vacated cars stripped along side the road and had to be careful of the drivers who were obviously all late for work. I thought I drove fast, whoa!!

Musically speaking and borrowing a line from one of Frank Sinatra's classics, 'if you can drive in New York, you can drive anywhere'. You have not seen crazy driving until you have been to New York. Once in the city I came to an intersection and saw my very first traffic policeman who directed traffic with his whistle. I sat mesmerized for a second taking everything in that was going at two times the speed of regular America. Then without the 'Minnesota nice', the policeman looked at me and yelled, "what the hell are you looking at? Get going". Thinking he might shoot me I applied my foot to the accelerator and left. I believe the name of the city we drove to, to pick up his wife and possessions was Jamaica. It was a concrete jungle with many people peering out of their windows looking into space with a spirit of hopelessness. This was so different than Minnesota. It made me appreciate where I came from.

Because I was the low man on the totem pole of experience I was assigned to the K1 and K8 departments of the lab. I was tasked with calibrating and repairing multi-meters and resistance measurement devices on base. All field equipment on base had a maintenance schedule and they would bring in the equipment for its periodic tune-up as well as dropping off anything that was not working properly. The most challenging part of the job was troubleshooting the defective pieces of equipment. I would open the blue print schematic of the broken piece of equipment and with the help of the operating manual investigate and try to discover which transistor, capacitor, chip or tube was defective. Like usual I did not fully appreciate the challenge of the job because I was not living in the moment and was always looking into the future. I was convinced my friends back home were having a great time and I was missing out. I would find out later that they may have had some fun times but they were individually going through their own growing pains and were trying to figure out who they were and what to do with their lives. For you young people out there take that as a piece of advice, the grass only seems greener on the other side of the fence.

I had three big events at work, one of which was very significant to me. The first one was a potential death experience. I had been there about six months when I decided to bring a little bit of weed to work and get high in the bathroom. I used my Binaca Blast breath spray to hide the smell in the bathroom as well as my breath. It would be the first and last time I would ever get high at work. I walked back to my area and connected this amp meter I was calibrating to our voltage and current standard. An amp meter measures electrical current and if you are not careful you can easily get electrocuted and get hurt. I made the connections and turned on the current standard. Zapppppp, I flew backwards a couple of feet with a small yelp. My supervisor came over to see if I was o.k. I told him I was alright. I thought for sure I was busted but he told me everyone of us has gotten zapped so be careful.

The next two events were one of failure and one of success. I had been lobbying for an opportunity to calibrate our labs gigantic two ton phase angle standard that is used to measure the polarity of AC sine waves. It was in my K8 section and it came up for its yearly diagnostic check. My supervisor said it was too complicated for me and that it has been a pain in the butt for the few people who have done it in the past. I pleaded with him to let me have a try. He changed his mind and gave me the opportunity. I went back into my work area and connected a signal generator and other resistant standards to the Phase Angle standard testing to see if it was within its range specifications. I signed off that it was working properly and waited. I knew my boss would perform the same diagnostics and would tell me if I was accurate on my assessment. He followed the same diagnostic checks and verified I had done the job completely and accurately. It was a monumental moment in my life that told me I have the ability to do many things when I put my mind behind it. I was on top of the mountain but I would also learn where there is a mountain there is also a valley.

I had a plan going into the USAF to get as much training as I could and then parlay that into a good job in the civilian sector after my four year commitment expired. I would be a hot commodity I thought. I would have the theoretical education and the hands on experience that would make me more valuable to a company than a person who just had the schooling. In my foolishness I had communicated that message to my military career colleagues. If you were them would you be so willing to help assist a young imprudent man who despises the very life you have embraced for a career? The answer is no. I had been working in the Chevy Nova department and I wanted to work with the Cadillac and sport car department. I finally got my chance. I was given an opportunity to troubleshoot an oscilloscope in the K3 frequency department. I tried and could not figure it out. One of the guys who worked in that area said something that cut me down to the bone. I was so hurt and demoralized that I went into the break room and started crying. I wanted so much to climb to the mountain peak again as well as earn the respect of my peers and I blew it.

Later that night as I was drowning in deep depression one of my married co-workers had knocked on my door to pay me a visit. His name was Rocky Sirois and he told me that everything was going to be o.k. and don't pay attention to what was said. He lifted my spirits and I went back to work the next day. It is amazing what a shot of encouragement can do to someone. Thank you Rocky! Speaking of Rocky, gives me an opportunity to say another nice thing about him. We played on a softball team together off base and I was privileged to watch him put on a line drive hitting show through out the weekend that almost single handily won the tournament we were playing in. He had one of those Michael Jordan 'zone' moments where the basket is as large as a bathtub.

The world continued to spin the sun kept rising every morning, and I kept counting down the days until August 7, 1987 when my four years were up. I made it to work everyday and continued to learn more and more. When work ended it was to the chow hall and then to the dorm. I found myself restless quite often and I hated my stay on the base. The base was in a very remote area up by the Canadian border and it was the antithesis of the places I had filled out on my 'dream sheet' at tech school. Besides softball I drank a lot of beer and smoked weed a few times. I could have smoked it more often but again the fear of a random urine test kept me mostly a beer drinker. To pass time on the weekend I went to the NCO Club periodically and on a couple of occasions I drove to a night club in Canada with a few friends. I thought I had a little groove in my boogie until I saw a troupe of break dancers from New York tearing it up on the dance floor.

Just like tech school I saw someone I knew get caught with marijuana and get kicked out of the Air Force. This time it was Don, the guy my age who came in a couple of months after me at my job. We initially did not get along at all, but as time went by we became friends. One night Don had went off base and went to a bar. When he arrived back at base the MP at the gate suspected he had too much to drink. He gave Don a sobriety test and searched his car. In his glove department the MP found a pot pipe. While Don was anxiously waiting to find out what they were going to do, I was anxiously waiting as well. Would Don tell any of the high ranking brass that he knew I and other people on base had smoked marijuana as well? The urine test for marijuana came back positive and five weeks later, Don was a civilian. It was sad to see him go. Our relationship had gone from adversarial to amicable. We didn't hang out with each other but when we saw each other it was enjoyable. It would be wonderful to find out that his life has been prosperous and joyful, and oh yeah, he never told on anyone.

If it were not for softball I may have went insane. I played for a team and found out that I was a pretty good softball player. I had a baseball background and if you think about it, how can't you be relatively good when the pitcher lobs an oversized baseball at you underhanded at changeup speed. This was the complete opposite of my last few years of baseball where I had my problems hitting the change up. It just so happens that this game that gave me something to look forward to and keep me busy and out of trouble, would also be the very thing that would have me write a letter to the base commander begging him to not kick me out but give me another chance.

I had neglected my electronic course studies that I was required to do and got behind. I was told to report to the base commander's office because he wanted to talk to me. I stood at attention in his office and he asked me why I was behind in my studies. The only excuse I had was that I was playing too much softball. After listening he gave me a direct order to stop playing softball until I was caught up in my studies. I said, "Yes sir", gave him a salute and went back to work. A week later the Commander was driving his base car when he drove by the softball field and saw me playing softball. I was at shortstop and when I saw his car I knew I was in trouble. Right after the game I went to my dorm room and started writing a letter. I gave the letter to my boss who delivered it to the Commander. A few weeks later I would get orders that I was going to Colorado for a two week course on 'radiation measurement equipment', and then from there I would be going to my new duty base. Again God gave me another chance instead of letting me have the consequences I deserved.

I flew out to Colorado and completed the radiac course. At the new base where I would be going I would be the person who would now be responsible for calibrating the radiation Geiger counter detectors. Did the commander try to set me up for radiation poisoning to exact his revenge? Nah, the person who was responsible where I would be reassigned had left and went to another base, thus creating a service need. After completing the radiation course in Colorado, I flew home for a couple of week's vacation before flying out over the ocean to trouble the next base commander at my new base. You would think that after I had narrowly escaped an early termination from the job that I was banking my future on as well as the hundreds of other things I had escaped from without harm, that I would have wised up and left the house on the hill, got into the car, drove down Stupid Lane and tried to get back on the safe lane before it was to late. Nah, I was GRAY with a pocketful of money ready to have a good time and all that I saw before me was the day that I was in.

CHAPTER 12

The Cat is Dead

On my second day back I asked Cory if I could borrow his car so I could drive a female friend and myself out to the Anoka county fair. In the car on our way home I had just finished smoking a joint. Immediately after putting the roach in the ashtray I noticed that I was in the left turn lane. I slid over into the right lane so I could continue to go forward and three seconds later boom. A car approaching from the opposite direction thought I was going to turn and thus they turned in front of me and we collided in the intersection. Fortune would have it that no one in either car was injured.

The next day I woke up to the sound of my brother screaming and going berserk by the side of the house. He had a sledgehammer and was standing on top of his car smashing the windows. To say he was not happy with the condition I brought his car home in would be an understatement. I knew there was only thing I could do to make amends and that was to buy him another car. So that day we went out and I bought him a car he liked that cost me around $750. It could have been much worse for me, ("Lizzie Borden took an axe and gave her mother forty whacks, when she saw what she had done, she gave her father forty-one") if you catch my drift. This would be my third vehicle accident and second one related to marijuana by the ashtray.

My first automobile accident happened on a beautiful summer day during summer vacation before the eleventh grade. Mulvey, Barrett and I were coming back from Lake Calhoun. I was driving my burgundy 1974 Grand AM. While traveling North on Hwy 100 we saw a pretty young lady on the other side of the highway walking along the frontage road going in the direction of 36th avenue. Thinking like young Italian fashion designers, we wanted to get a closer look at her clothes ensemble. I turned onto 36th Ave. and drove up to a cross street to turn around. As I slowed down to turn I decided to keep going instead. This fooled the motorcycle behind me who laid his bike down and skidded into my back bumper. In a panic just like I did when I got hit by a car as a six year old, my first instinct was to run. So I hit the gas and took off. One second later I heard a yell and hit the brakes because the guy and his bike were now an appendage of my rear bumper. I had no damage to my car but his motorcycle was scratched up pretty good, so he took me to a small claims court and sued me for damages.

For my defense I had brought Mulvey with me. Our plan was to simply stand in front of the judge and tell it like it wasn't. Mike with his angelic innocent looking face (Mike looked exactly like Ralphie from the 1983 movie 'Christmas Story') told the judge what he saw from his vantage point in the backseat. What he said and what he saw did not exactly match. The judge was swayed somewhat and gave me a lower at fault % than I would have received without his testimony. Because I didn't have insurance I had to sell my pimp mobile to pay for his bike.

About a year later I got into another car accident. This would be the first of my ashtray accidents. I had just picked up a bag of weed from my dealer and was heading home. While driving I was admiring the bag of weed and dreaming of the moment I would be killing my brain cells. I was holding the bag down by the ashtray so no other drivers could see; hence the ashtray accident denominator. Just as soon as I started looking at the bag of weed a car that was sitting in a left turn lane decided at the last second to go forward and turned into my lane. Whether I could have avoided him if I wasn't distracted I don't know, but I braked and crashed into the rear of his car, totaling my 1969 Dodge Coronet I bought from Duane's Auto; also known as Honest Al. Like the time before, I didn't have insurance but this time the fault of the accident was all credited to the other driver. I abandoned the car on the street across from Target, pocketed my bag of weed and walked home. The days of having my own vehicle were over until I purchased a lemon from my bosses' boss at Loring AFB, the real deal Honest Al. It lasted two weeks before the engine died.

The day came for me to leave home and go to my next duty base. The name of my new home was Lajes Air Field, Azores. This was a small island out in the Atlantic Ocean which was governed by the country of Portugal. My mother thought it would be helpful for me to take one of her prescription Valium to calm my nerves. I can see why it was the most abused prescription drug in America at the time. I arrived at the base without a care in the world and stepped out of the plane into a tropically hot and humid sauna. I went from one isolated remote base to another one opposite only in temperature. My vision of the Azores did not match the reality of the Azores. I was a little disappointed. The pretty name gave me the impression of a tropical island surrounded by white sandy beaches laced with palm trees and rain forest fauna. Instead it was mostly rocky along the coast with only two sand beaches on the whole island. When it wasn't humid in the summer it was windy and rainy in the winter.

I was taken to my new dorm room at the barracks. There were about sixteen rooms on each of the three floors. Each floor had a community room, laundry room, kitchen and bathroom/shower. My room was on the first floor in the barracks that was on top of the hill about ¾ of a mile from the islands cliff edge. It was cool to look out at the blue ocean that stretched out as far as the horizon but a few months later that same ocean seemed like a fence that kept me imprisoned on the island. I arrived on a Saturday and went to my new job on Monday.

The lab was about three miles from the barracks on the edge of the island. Periodically one of the local Azorean sheepherders would pass their flock of sheep or their gaunt cows along side our building. This is not something you would see on a military base in America. My first day there I was introduced to everyone including my new boss who was a Sr. Master Sergeant. He told me that he was aware of my discipline at my other base and would not hold any bias against me. I was at a new base with a fresh start he said. It was a beautiful gesture on his part but about two weeks later I would have him scratching his head and thinking 'what have I inherited from the other base'.

Like I said about two weeks later one of the guys I worked with named Rob said he wanted to take me off base and show me some of the island. We left the base in a taxicab and drove down to the nearest town. We ate at one of the small restaurants that served this delicious octopus stew and beef dish. From there we danced around town popping in and out of a couple of taverns. We drank beer and had a merry old time. Rob introduced me to a thick green licorice tasting Portuguese liqueur called Anis. He convinced me to drink a few shots and I obliged him even though I could not stomach the taste.

Generally speaking there is nothing but "no good" going on after midnight, so Rob and I should have called it quits. We had to be at work in 8 hours and would be better equipped to do our job if we had the proper amount of rest, (teaching moment for young people). Instead we decided to go to the beach and continue the party. It was a beautiful night with stars shining brightly above and the ocean rolling its small waves up to the shore. I had decided that it would be a waste not to jump in and go swimming.

Years later I would give God a belated "thank you" for saving my life. God only knows how many times in my life that I had the one set of footprints in the sand. This was one of them. I was about 15 feet out from shore when I got caught in a riptide. As I began to swim I realized that the water was pulling me backwards preventing me from returning to the beach. So I began to swim harder and harder. I never heard of a riptide nor knew that I should swim diagonally to shore when caught in one. Soon the adrenaline from my panic kicked in. With all of the strength I had and a lot of help from my over worked guardian angel, I made it back to shore where I collapsed in sheer exhaustion. Five minutes later after catching my breath, I put my pants and shirt back on and sat on the beach. Rob had called for a taxi and when that arrived we went back to the base.

It was around 1:00 in the morning when we got back and I was sicker than a dog. I threw up in the bathroom and then I went into the six man shower unit and lay on the floor with the water raining down on me for about 30 minutes. Eventually I got up and went to my room. The morning came and there was a knock on my door. Rob had knocked on my door telling me to get up and get ready to go to work. I told him I wasn't going to work. He left and about an hour later I had another knock on the door, this time it was from a mid grade sergeant who was in charge of my barracks. I told him I was getting up so he would go. He left and I continued to lie in bed. I guess about a half hour later, there was another knock on the door and then the door was unlocked and the big boss from work was there. He told me to get up, get dressed and he would drive me to work.

When we arrived at work we were told that the base commander wanted to see the both of us in his office. We drove down there and I was still feeling like garbage. He went in first and I sat out in the outer part of the office. While I was sitting out there I knew that the only thing that would save me from getting kicked out of the service was for me to tell him I had a drinking problem and that I needed help. It was the only card I had left to play. I went in to the Commander's office and told him that. He told me to go grab a seat outside of his door and that he was going to talk to my boss again. While I was sitting outside the door I overheard the commander saying to my boss that either I am very smart or I really did have a drinking problem. He wanted to give me discipline which I believe would have been a discharge, but was now obligated to get me some help. The Colonel couldn't nail me on this but about fourteen months later he would have an opportunity to stick me and he would. I wound up having to go to a weekly Alcoholics Anonymous type help group for about eight weeks. While this is going on Rob my co-worker who took me out for a night of drinking would get nailed on a urine test for marijuana. He was booted out and I believe he received a dishonorable discharge. That made three military bases I was stationed at and three people I worked with who got kicked out for marijuana usage.

My first roommate was named Marty. He was a nice jovial chap who stood all of 5 feet tall if that and was built like a 180 lb bowling ball. It the Air Force was the brains of the Military as we considered ourselves and not the brawn, then Marty was proof in the pudding for the non-brawn category. After living with him, watching other Airmen and rehashing my life, the brains designation maybe undeserved. Marty worked the graveyard shift and I worked the morning hours from 7:00- 3:30 pm. We saw each other in passing which made it easy to have an amicable relationship. Like most single men in the armed services, alcohol was part of his diet as well. A few months later he would leave and go back to the states leaving me with a room to myself, something I treasured. A month after Marty left I would have the first of my three temporary roommates.

Troy was from the west coast; Alex was from the east coast and Dave somewhere in the middle. Troy Donaldson was from Sacramento, California and was one year older than me. He arrived on base about three weeks earlier than his wife so he roomed with me until she came over. Because he was able to get an assignment closer to home, he would only stay at Lajes Air Field for about six months. Troy was a joy to know. He was funny and had a great sense of humor. While he was on base we became best of friends. Years after we both were discharged from the Air Force, we sent a few Christmas cards to each other, talked on the phone once and then became preoccupied with our own families. When Troy left the Lajes Air Field to go back to a base in California, he gave me his old VW bug for a discounted price. Cars had to be flown in from the states and you had to pay a premium price to get one over. Most guys did not have a car including myself. Because of that, most time was spent on base.

After Troy moved back to California my next roommate was Alex from New York City. Alex loved his music and periodically spun records at the NCO club. After Alex moved out to his own room a few months later I would have the last of my roommates. His name was Dave and like Troy and Alex, he was married and also a very nice guy. Where Alex was all hip-hop, Dave was all hard rock/metal music. Every day after work with no exception, he came back to the room, listened to music and drank Jack Daniels until he fell asleep.

On one occasion around 7:00 pm, Dave had passed out on his bed from drinking. I went over and changed the time on his alarm clock and then set his alarm to go off at the time he would wake up to go to work. The alarm went off and he woke up very, very groggy. He looked at the clock and his brain began to spin. He couldn't believe it was morning time and that he had to get up. He asked me if this was the right time and I told him yes. He asked me a few more times and I said yes again. He crawled off his bed and slowly walked out of the room down the hall to take a shower. After his shower he came back to the room still groggy and drunk. There was no calling in sick or being late for him because he worked for the Base Commander in his office. After getting nice and spiffy, he went to leave and walked out the door. About two minutes later he came back in hotter than an egg on a highway in Texas in the middle of July. It took him awhile but he figured it out. Since my joke was not appreciated I made a decision to deprive him of my presence and left. Later that night I tip-toed back in when he was asleep.

Work continued to go smoothly with very few bumps along the way. I was given opportunities to calibrate and repair some of the more advanced electronic test equipment in the field. Some of the items were oscilloscopes, signal generators and spectrum analyzers. In addition to that, the Radiac School I went to before coming over put me in sole position of checking all radiation measuring equipment that came into the lab. I had a little amount of pride knowing that I was the only one on base who was skilled and certified to verify that all radiation measurement equipment was working within their proper operating specifications.

When work ended the highlight of my day was getting out playing softball when softball season was in session. I loved to play and was selected as lone representative from our team to play in the Base All STARS game. The wind was blowing out that day and I hit a home run in my only plate appearance. In the fall I was the quarterback for our flag football team. We were a middle of the road team, but our highlight came when we beat the grunts; the Army team. I had my best day, throwing for four touchdowns and running for two more.

Sports did not fill all of my time though I wish it would have. I gambled periodically and at least one other person besides Stu who kept losing his money to me did not like it. One of the people in my barracks came up to me and told me that the commander knows your gambling and is watching. I said o.k. and took that as a warning to quit. It was around this time that I was accused of going into someone's room and stealing money. I believe my gambling and living on the same floor as the victim made me suspect number one. I was asked at work by the military police if I knew who may have done it. I told them no, but they did not believe me. They asked me if I would be willing to take a lie detector test. I said sure, so they hooked me up to the machine and asked me some questions. I passed like I knew I would but I was angry for even being a suspect. I might do knucklehead stuff but I was not a thief. I had officially retired from relocating other people's property after getting caught stealing that case of beer in 12th grade.

It brought back memories of the other time in my life when I was asked to take a lie detector test to prove my un-involvement in a small fire that happened in my stairwell in the projects I lived in off of Bass Lake Rd in 1977. The Fire Chief of New Hope was the father of a friend I had in fifth grade. Long story short……. I took the test and passed. I was angry and told myself I would never do that again, only to do it seven years later.

Besides killing time with gambling, I played Dungeons & Dragons. That only lasted a short while and came to an end when Troy left the island as well as Stu the Dungeon Master. Troy and I would play that game on every occasion we could. One time we were in my room playing and there was a knock on my door. It was his wife Betsy who had been running around looking for him. She found him and was quite angry that he had been dodging her. Betsy and Troy would get a divorce a couple years later.

Minus the seasonal sports that I played a few times a week and my infrequent gambling, most of my time was spent hanging around the barracks drinking beer with the other lounge lizards. I had an opportunity to take college courses and grow academically but I was extremely short sighted. If only I had wisdom back then to realize that time is a finite quantity allotted to each of us, and what we do with that time will make life worth living in that moment and in the future.

The old saying that a cat has nine lives could have been said about me in the military. I did many things that would have justified being discharged and somehow I had managed to stay one step ahead of the reaper. I was living in my ninth life on Columbus Day 1986 when the grim reaper finally caught me. The weather on that day was beautiful. It was a perfect day to drive around the island in my blue Volkswagen bug on the cobblestone streets and sight see. Dan Dicenzo and I picked up a 12 pack of Budweiser and started drinking around 11:00 in the morning. We continued through the day up to 12:00 midnight.

After leaving one of the local night clubs we decided to go back to base to get something to eat at the mess hall. Not being able to see a painted directional area on the road, I had pulled into a parking lot exit and drove out of the parking lot entrance in my attempt to turn around. A military police car happened to see me pull out of the entrance and pulled me over in our barracks parking lot. I got out and the MP gave me a sobriety test which I am absolutely convinced I passed. He arrested me and took me to the station for a urine test. My boss at work was called and he came to the station and picked me up. As much as I had to drink in the past twelve hours I felt very sober. For the next week at work I was on pins and needles waiting for the urine results. I was convinced that I was going to get nailed for having THC in my system because about three weeks prior I had smoked some weed. I was thinking I was going to receive a dishonorable discharge and kill my chances of getting a good job back home.

I was told to report to the Commander and he told me that he was going to discharge me from the USAF. I was going to be kicked out because I was charged with a D.U.I.

The blood alcohol test came back with a measured level of .07%. Back home in the states anything under .10 is legal, but in the Azores anything above .05 is illegal. I was flabbergasted that the % was that low. I was very sad but relieved that it was not due to marijuana usage. Instead of a dishonorable discharge I could have received, I was going to receive a 'General under Honorable' discharge. The Colonel finally got to do what he wanted to do to me in my second week on base; and I finally got what I deserved. Eighteen days later I was a civilian flying back home to Minneapolis, Minnesota.

I look back on my military experience with mixed emotions. I had shame and regret for my immature attitude and the many actions I committed that were wrong. A rose is beautiful, but so are lilies, tulips and the thousand other kinds. Because I grew up in a 99% white ethnic neighborhood I was deprived of the richness of diversity. I met and saw many different types of people (flowers) in the USAF and this gave me much joy and enlarged my perspective on life.

    I arrived at the Mpls/St Paul International Airport happy to finally be back home for good and free from my military obligation, but somber because I had been kicked out. Only losers get kicked out of the military I thought, and now I was one of them. Waiting there for me with a big smile was mom. We hugged and then we walked to the baggage carousel to get my luggage and then go home. On the way home as she was driving, I was taking in the sites of the city thinking and feeling the same thing Dorothy said when she was clicking her ruby red shoes in the Wizard of Oz, "there is no place like home". From the first moment I had left to go into the Air Force I was continually thinking about getting out and being back home. Two and a half years into my four year commitment I had sent out a few letters to a couple of electronic firms in Minnesota telling them about my education and training and seeing if there were any opportunities for employment. I received a letter back saying thank you for the interest but not at this time. I was finally home, now what?

    After relaxing for a few days I went down to the USPS and applied. Because I had a 'general under honorable conditions' discharge from the military I had a four month window to apply and test. Normally it would open up to the public every two to four years and thousands of people would apply and compete for a handful of jobs. I was hoping for a job, but since I was not sure I would get hired I began to study for my electronics FCC license. My plan was to acquire my FCC license which would put me in a good position to get an electronic tech job. Before that happened I was called by the USPS in February and after taking the entrance exam I was hired as a career employee in April. I laid aside my electronic tech aspiration and became a mail clerk.

    One year after I was discharged from the USAF, I moved into my very own place in the city of Brooklyn Park with my own bed in my own bedroom. My mom had sacrificially given up her bed for me after I got out of the USAF and she slept on a cot in the living room of her apartment. She made it as comfortable for me as she could and now she finally had her bed back. She did not have much, but whatever she had she always was willing to give.

    I moved into my first apartment with a girl a few years younger than me whom I had met a month before. She did not have a job so she was unable to contribute any money towards rent, food or the utilities. What she did not provide in the form of money she gave to me with cuddles on the couch and in bed. She was beautiful with short hair and had a playful crazy spirit, something I enjoyed. Her name was Tchaikovsky and she was my cat. Boris the husband of my mom's best friend found her in an abandoned house and I welcomed her into my house thinking she was a he; hence the man's name. When I would come home from work she would be there waiting for me. She would hunch her back and walk sideways towards me with a tough guy look in her eyes asking the question "where the heck have I been for the past nine hours"? I would bat at her with my hand and she would bat back with her paw. Even though I was 40 times her weight and had her by 63 inches she thought she could take me. I would go at her and she would counter with the 'rope a dope' from Muhammad Ali and then lunge at my ear like a little Mike Tyson. After 15 rounds of boxing it would end in a split decision and she would win again.

One time when I had company over she got real excited and ran up the guests' pants legs and then did a u-turn at the shoulder going down the other leg. It was quite funny but with her claws it was a little painful. I know that because she did it to me a couple of times. Our time together would be short because I had my head up my butt again. I came home from work and saw that she manicured her nails on the mesh screen of my new three foot speakers. I got so mad that I put her in the car and drove her up to the Animal Humane Society. The following day I realized how foolish I was and how much I missed her. I went back up to the humane society to get her back, but she was gone. Someone had went there looking for a cat and found a treasure.

During this period of time my work schedule had me starting at 5:00 in the afternoon and working till 1:30 in the morning with two hours of mandatory overtime usually given on Friday and Saturday nights. The one day I did work during the day was on Sunday and that was at 12:00 which ruined the whole day. To say I hated this schedule would be an understatement. The only time I could go out with my friends was to call in sick and I became pretty good at it. This eventually got me into trouble and lead to a few suspensions. I was inching closer to getting fired. I was making another mess in my life and did not know where to turn for answers, or what to do. What was my purpose? What did the future hold for me? Why am I unhappy? Why am I gray?

CHAPTER 13

Amazing Grace

"The God who made the world and everything in it is the Lord of heaven and earth does not live in temples built by hands. And he is not served by human hands, as if he needed anything, because he himself gives all men life and breath and everything else. From one man he made every nation of men that they should inhabit the whole earth; and he determined the times set for them and the exact places where they should live. God did this so that men would seek him and perhaps reach out for him and find him, though he is not far from each one of us." (Acts 17:24-27)

Are there places in the world that are better to be born than others? From a human perspective the answer to this question is proportionately related to many factors such as the availability and opportunity for education, healthcare, safety, leisure and jobs. They are good and legitimate reasons but not the chief reason from God's standpoint. God has judiciously placed the human spirit into every baby at various geographic spots in the world. My understanding of the love of God, tells me that each spot regardless of how bad the parents are, how poor the country is, ect., is something God deemed the best place of opportunity for that person to seek himself. America in my opinion is the greatest country in the world, but because of its affluence, it has bowed down to worship at the altar of entertainment and has lost its sensitivity to hear the saving call of the Spirit of God.

I would be pretentious to suggest that I understand all or most of what God does. I do believe that his written word is true and reflects clearly his desire for everyone born. As a shepherd calling and looking for his lost sheep, so is God calling to everyone who is lost that they may find the good pasture that provides for all of their needs and gives REST to their soul. *"Come to me, all you who are weary and burdened, and I will give you rest. Take my yoke upon you and learn from me, for I am gentle and humble in heart, and you will find rest for your souls. For my yoke is easy and my burden is light." (Matt 11:28-30)*

In the early months of 1988 I began to experience a restlessness I could not understand. I lived in a nice apartment, had a good paying job with good benefits, and had good health but was very empty inside. Some of the cause of that emptiness was found in me changing, and my childhood friends changing. Our trains had left the train station moving in different directions. I began to spend time with other people, but they were in essence stop gap friends. Across the hall I had befriended a married couple who must have had an arranged marriage set up before they were born, (their names purposely omitted). Their marriage was ugly and would end in divorce. One night late in the morning with her and her sister-in-law over my house drinking, I made an ill-advised pass towards her. The next morning there was a knock on my door with her standing there. She told me she had an affair once before and would be willing to have an affair with me if I wanted too. My want for female companionship was as large as every other young man in the world but I awkwardly told her no. In my heart I knew one of the pieces missing was that special woman to share life with but not under these circumstances. I also sensed something bigger than that was missing in my life, but I could not put my finger on it.

I was very happy to have a job working for the USPS, but it was not very satisfying. I figured everything in life centered around a persons job, so if I had to start somewhere it probably should be at work. The thought of working independently, having an adjustable schedule with an open ceiling of revenue opened my eyes up to becoming a realtor. So I meandered over to the library and checked out a bunch of books about realty and realtors. About three weeks later my AA battery passion for becoming a realtor lost all of its charge and I turned my attention towards physical conditioning. A professional athlete was the prize and I decided I was going to be a boxer or the missing piece of the Minnesota Vikings team; their needed halfback. I might have gotten knocked out by Thomas 'the Hitman' Hearns, 'Marvelous' Marvin Hagler, or Sugar Ray Leonard, but losing to Darrin Nelson, no way! I began to exercise and after a few weeks the alarm went off and I woke up from my dream. There was no way on God's green planet that I was going to get in the door of any of those professions let alone pull into the driveway while I was smoking dope every day. Besides it's hard to get in real great shape when you have the munchies all of the time. During this time mom thought I was losing it, and she had every reason to think this. I look back and just laugh. I joke that I was also contemplating going down to NASA to become an astronaut.

A few weeks after I had quit training and had drifted back into my familiar dead hole, I stumbled across a bible in my apartment. How it got there I do not remember. I never read from the bible before and only went to church a few times in my life. I began to read the bible vigorously and the emptiness inside me started to dissipate. I began to learn about who I was even though I wasn't even asking the question. I found out that I was first created in the mind of God sometime back in eternity past. This God had created me and all of mankind in his image which meant that I/we have the ability to reason, love, appreciate, laugh, cry, imagine, think abstract, formulate ideas, serve others, feel compassion, hate evil, comprehend justice, be merciful, and offer forgiveness.

I also learned that all of humanity was given free will to make decisions including the most important decision of whether to believe and embrace Jesus as Lord and Savior. Robots or beings that are forced to love, is not love. It has to be voluntary and willful, and that is why God gave mankind free-will. One of the inherent qualities of God is that he is Love. He loves to love and he loves to be loved. He has revealed himself to all of humanity through the course of time in nature, our conscience, the written word, the lives of transformed people and God incarnate himself; Jesus. The bible says mankind will be without excuse and no person will be able to say they didn't have an opportunity to know him.

Each person is pursued by God no matter where they are located in the world. God has placed within everyone's heart/mind awareness that there is a God. When people begin to respond to the prodding of God through the Holy Spirit, he (God) brings them closer to himself culminating in 100% awareness and the opportunity to have a personal relationship. The longer a person continues to snub the prodding of God they can develop a callousness which will result in decreased sensitivity and awareness; thus they will never see the truth of who they are and who Jesus is. Finally the sad truth, everyone who chooses to reject a relationship with Jesus will be eternally separated and will suffer indescribable agony because they will have been guilty of the greatest crime in the universe. Their agony will be self inflicted as they will forever have the guilt of rejecting the love of God and living without forgiveness for their lifetime of sin.

The place where people will go who reject Jesus is called hell and God does not want one person to go there. (John 3:16)

Here is what the great American theologian Jonathan Edwards had to say about God, mankind's responsibility to him, and God's right to discipline. "Our obligation to love, honor, and obey any being, is in proportion to his loveliness, honorableness, and authority; for that is the very meaning of the words. But God is a being infinitely lovely, because he has infinite excellency and beauty. To have infinite excellency and beauty is the same thing as to have infinite loveliness. He is a being of infinite greatness, majesty, and glory; and therefore he is infinitely honorable. He is infinitely exalted above the greatest potentates of the earth, and highest angels in heaven; and therefore he is infinitely more honorable than they. His authority over us is infinite; and the ground of his right to our obedience is infinitely strong; for he is infinitely worthy to be obeyed himself, and we have an absolute, universal, and infinite dependence upon him. So that sin against God, being a violation of infinite obligations, must be a crime infinitely heinous, and so deserving of infinite punishment."

I do not remember the day or less the month that I started reading the bible, but I know I kept on reading it. They say that most people who begin to read the bible and later become Christians do so because there was someone in their life encouraging them and/or living out a lifestyle in front of them that was attractive and/or made them feel lacking by comparison. I didn't have either and I find that absolutely amazing. As I began to read I began to change slowly. This one example is for the boys out there who can relate. I was reading about lusting in the bible and I sadly admit was a world class luster. I worked in the same area with this beautiful lady my age who wore tight jeans everyday. The temptation was too hard to resist and everyday I and every other male gawked.

In this particular week my mind was saturated with the bible and I had zero impulses to look at the brand name sewn on the backside of her jeans. I was amazed. I felt a purity that I never felt before. I tasted the power of God's holiness and I loved it. To my shame I have succumbed to that lustful spirit more times than I want to admit up to this present day. Christians are not sinless. We sin less and in some of the days of our life we re-visit some of our old and ugly habits. The bible says we will wrestle periodically until the day when we are changed completely. I am not perfect yet but I thank God I am not the same person I was.

Ask a Christian when they asked Jesus to come into their life and most will tell you about an event or even a specific day. I cannot do that.

I just remember reading, and reading, and changing and changing. The changes that occurred and have continued in my life are changes that I believe are signs of a genuine encounter and 'born again' experience every true believer should manifest. Not in any order of rank, but I will list and describe some of the changes that have happened to me.

- Thankful and joyful spirit: I have an attitude of gratitude that has spilled over into my life when I think of what God has done for me (past and present), and for his future promises. The jealous or envious spirit that I occasionally had has been replaced with happiness for others when they are recipients of something good, including things that I would have liked to have received.
- Concerned spirit:
My preoccupation with self has lessened and my awareness to the pains of others including their needed relationship with God has increased. This has spurned in me an action of prayer and helpful involvement in their lives.
- Willing spirit:
The old saying "it's the thought that counts" does not apply to a follower of Jesus. I have been changed inside to want to help people. This has been heightened since becoming a Christian.
- Desiring God's will:
Going to church on Sunday is not the all in all. I have a daily desire to please God. Some days are harder than others as I continue to fight the old man who still lives within me.
- Humility:
"Do nothing out of selfish ambition or vain conceit, but in humility consider others better than yourselves". (Phil 2:3) Even though I consider myself the best gamer in the world, I do not laud it over anyone except maybe Tom.
- Bold spirit:
The bible says anyone who is ashamed of him (Jesus) has no part with him in heaven. If Jesus is who he says he is and he did what the bible said he did, he is without doubt worthy of acknowledging and talking about. What would cause the twelve disciples who lived and walked with him for three years to suffer persecution, rejection and alienation from family and community, and then to willingly accept death as a martyr, unless it were not true? I am a Jesus Freak and proud of it.

- Holiness:
  'But just as he who called you is holy, so be holy in all you do; for it is written, 'Be holy, because I am holy'. (1Pet 1:15,16) I am a work in progress.

CHAPTER 14

The Girl from Siam

It was during this time of soul searching and bible reading that Lolita the daughter of a cousin of Claire's had popped over my apartment for a visit to tell me that I had to meet this girl that she knew who lived up the street by her. Her birth name was Rome Faengrathok and she was born in Bangkok, Thailand in 1966 during the Vietnam War. She was nicknamed Apple as a baby and it stuck until she died. Her mothers name was Piak, and Piak was a bar girl/ prostitute who had gotten pregnant by a black G.I. The six years that Apple and I were married, I only saw Piak a handful of times. She had nothing to do with Apple and only visited her grandkids one time that I remember. It was not until Apple acquired stomach cancer in 1998 that Piak involved herself in the life of Apple and her grandkids. After Apple's death she would visit periodically and bring presents for all of the kids including her step grandkid Rico. Piak was a cheerful lady who always had a smile. I had a strong dislike for her when Apple was alive because she had distanced herself from Apple and her grandkids, but that changed when she made the decision to be a grandma and enter the lives of her grandkids. I grew to love and enjoy her.

A few years after Apple's death she took me, Vonda and the kids on a three day vacation to Wisconsin Dells, the world's largest water theme park in the country. It was her treat but Vonda and I were the ones who paid for everything because she was maxed out on her credit cards. She promised to pay us back but never did. It was o.k. because we all had a very good time. Piak would get divorced from Mike V. and marry another man around the time I had met Apple. After Apples death Piak got divorced again. She moved back to Thailand and bought a house. She stayed in touch by calling on the holidays and the kids' birthdays to say hi and that she loved everyone. A couple of years later she called me sobbing uncontrollably. She was in a financial mess and wanted to come back to America. She didn't tell me that but a few years later someone told me that she had lost all of her money gambling. This was something that had plagued her in both of her marriages. She asked if I would help her try to get back to the United States. I said I would, but I knew there was nothing I could do except console and encourage her. The last time I would talk to her was a little before the great tsunami of 2004 hit Thailand and killed thousands of people.

Apple was raised by her grandmother and lived with a few cousins. Piak was ashamed of Apple though she never said it. My belief why she shunned her own daughter was because Apple was very dark skinned and was a walking, talking billboard that broadcasted to the world that her mother was a prostitute, and had sex with a black man. About five years later Apple's mother met an U.S. Army guy stationed in Bangkok named Mike V. They got married and Piak moved to the United States. Mike said to me that he saw Apple around but never knew where she fit in the Faengrathok clan. It was not until five years later back home in Minnesota that Mike found out Apple was Piaks' daughter.

Apple grew up very poor and in a similar but different way was gray like myself. We both had no father that claimed us; we both had mothers who violated the social taboo of having sexual relations with a black man outside of their race, and we both were looked upon like Rudolph the red nosed reindeer by some family members and some people in society. There is no blending in with the masses and being inconspicuous when your physical features blinked red. Apple told me the short story of when she and a girlfriend were sitting on the railroad tracks around the age of thirteen. Thailand is predominately a Buddhist country and this is what Apple was raised to believe. As they were talking, Apple was gazing up into the sky. She asked her friend if she thought there was a God. They mused on it for awhile and then went about their usual business. Exactly what Apple was asking is a direct result of (Psalm 19:1-4). *"The heavens declare the glory of God; the skies proclaim the work of his hands. Day after day they pour forth speech; night after night they display knowledge. There is no speech or language where their voice is not heard. Their voice goes out into all the earth, their words to the ends of the world."* Twenty years later she would bow her knee to him.

Apple knew only a little English and had a hard time learning the language and making the cultural adjustment when she came to America.

About a year after she arrived she took a city bus to the airport with the intentions of flying back to Thailand. At the ticket counter she put all of her money on the counter to buy an airline ticket but came up a few dollars short. She went back home very sad not knowing that God had a plan for her here in Minnesota. She continued going to Park Center high school and working part time waiting for her Prince Charming.

I called Apple and asked if she would like to go out to a movie. She said yes, so we set a day and time for our first date. Apple lived about two miles from me and was living with her step dad Mike. Mike is a great guy whom I enjoy being around. Also living at Mike's house with Apple was Apple's friend Delana or Danielle as she was more commonly called. I was invited in the house and I, Delana and Apple sat around the kitchen table and made small talk. Apple had met Delana at work and they had struck up a friendship. Delana asked Apple if she could help her out by allowing her to live with her at her mom and dads house for a little while until she found another place to live. Apple wanted to help so she asked her stepdad Mike if Delana could move in and Mike said yes. Delana had been living with her for about two months already.

My first impression of Apple was she was very shy and an attractive girl. After visiting with her and mostly her friend Delana, we left about thirty minutes later to go on my first date in four years. We hoped into my car and drove to the Terrace movie theatre in Robbinsdale. After the movie I invited her back to my apartment and one thing led to another and we engaged in marital activities. It was wonderful to have female companionship other than a cat but I knew in my heart we were not soulmates for one another. If I had any experience or any wisdom in dating I would not have chosen the movie/ apartment date for our first date. It should have been entirely a social get to know you date instead of what turned into a romantic evening.

You may think that Apple was some loose girl, but she told me that she was not that at all. She had only been with another man once before and continually fended off advances towards her when she went out dancing before I met her. She said that when she saw me she was quite smitten and that when I told her I was born in January she thought back to what her grandma told her. Her grandma had told her that she would meet and marry a guy who was born in January. It was unmistakable to me that Apple had fallen for me after only one date. I knew I had to end this relationship immediately with some form of respect to her.

The following day I went over to her house and told her I felt we were not meant to be together. I apologized and then left. The next day Lolita rang my buzzer and told me that Apple had placed some roses on my car and was hoping that I would change my mind. It was a beautiful gesture and I was a softy. We became boyfriend/girlfriend and she moved in a few weeks later. A few months later as we were lounging around the apartment, we were talking about something and I happened to tell her that someone I knew was going to propose to their girlfriend on Valentine's Day. Apple made a comment that I would never want her as my wife. I had brought up the marriage word for the first time in our relationship and she wanted to know if I felt the same way she did.

I had seen my mother used and abused by a few of her boyfriends and I had told myself I never wanted to be like those men. It dawned on me that I had all of the benefits of marriage without the commitments. I realized it was morally wrong of me to keep her on the hook until another fish swam along. I knew she was in love with me, so I leaned over to her and asked her if she would marry me. She said I was only asking her that because I was high. I told her that I loved her and I was not asking her to marry me because I was high. She happily accepted and we became engaged to be married. The next day we went out to look for a ring.

Sometime after our engagement Apple started a new job at the Walgreens drug store in the strip mall on Brooklyn Blvd and Zane Ave. Since I was working the grave yard shift at the post office she decided to work the 10:00 pm-6:30 am shift so we could be on the same schedule. After her car died, I began to pick her up on my way home from work. It must have been the second or third day when I pulled up to the curb in front of the store when I saw her standing outside waiting for me crying. She got into the car and I asked her what had happened, what was wrong. She would not tell me. I asked her again and then she told me the story.

Somewhere in the early morning hours, Apple was in the back storage room getting some pop to stock out front. All of a sudden and out of nowhere there appeared a man who started talking to her. Within seconds of him talking, Apple had dropped the tray of pop she was holding out of fright. The man disappeared and Apple ran out of the backroom to the pharmacist who was the only other person on duty in the store. Apple told him what she had seen and asked if he had seen anybody. He said no, so they both walked out into the mall corridor in front of the store and asked the mall security guard if he had seen anyone come out of the store and/or walk through the mall corridor in the last minute. He was an older guy who had been working that job for a few years. After Apple retold the account and described what the person looked like, the security guard said "whoa, the guy you just described was the store manager of Walgreens who committed suicide a few years back." Apple lost it and was an emotional wreck up to the time I picked her up. We went home, went to sleep and woke up for another day.

A night or two later Apple had another encounter with a man who had rattled her like the backroom episode. The man approached Apple in the early morning hours when no one else was in the store. If this person (demon) was masquerading as the manager who committed suicide I do not remember. He had asked for a pack of cigarettes and a roll of film. Apple said she could not look up at the man in his face or place the change into his hand. Both of which she did on every customer exchange. After he walked away, she hustled out of the store entrance and looked in both directions down the corridor for the man. She saw nothing. I cannot remember how Apple was when I picked her the second time, but I know she was unsettled because I told her I was going to buy her a necklace with a cross. We went home and after I woke up I went to the jewelry store and bought her a necklace with a cross.

My immediate response to the first encounter and ones thereafter, was Apple was being victimized by fallen angels (demons). I can only speculate why she was seeing them. My understanding is that most visible/ audible demon encounters happen through the occult and mind altering drugs. Apple never did drugs in her life so this did not apply to her; also she was not in the occult. Second, Apple was a non practicing Buddhist who was learning about Jesus through me. She had grown up in a Buddhist country and for her whole life she had been taught Buddhism is truth. The one true God in the world was going to break down the Buddhist walls of lies like Ronald Reagan broke down the East Berlin wall of evil the communists of Russia had built.

I believe the only logical explanation that answers the 'what', 'who', and 'why' of what she saw is found in how it ends. Apple would be introduced in a tangible and powerful way to the God she had wondered existed when she was a young girl. At this time I am a young Christian growing in my new faith. I told her that if this happens again, I want you to grab the cross and say "Jesus help me" or "In the name of Jesus I command you to leave." It was something in those terms. I am not certain if it was the same day I gave her the cross necklace, but Apple's third and final visitation happened very soon after. On this night, Apple had gone into the back store room for something. She was not back there for more than a couple of seconds when the original guy appeared behind her and to the side. As soon as he started talking Apple grabbed the cross around her neck and squeezed it tight. She said what I had told her to say and immediately the guy disappeared. Apple had no other episodes after that but decided it was not where she wanted to be. She quit working there a few weeks later and found a day job as a shoe salesperson at KMART. To my dismay and bewilderment, I would scratch my head many times in the following years while we were married never understanding why she did not embrace Jesus as Lord and Savior after he displayed his love and power towards her.

CHAPTER 15

Marriage and the Angel

On June 30, 1989 Apple and I were married. We were married in the courthouse judge's chamber and it had none of the trappings or feel of a traditional church wedding. I did not know it at the time but our sterile low key wedding would be a snapshot of our marriage; not much fanfare or excitement and partially business like. In attendance were my mother, Cory, Piak, Mike V. and Apple's friend Lynn.

Growing up as a kid I had two streams of input that painted a picture of what marriage was about. There was the comical television stream of Fred & Wilma Flintstone, Edith & Archie Bunker, George & Wheezy Jefferson, Hermann & Lily Munster and Robert & Carol Brady of the Brady Bunch. With the exception of Robert Brady all of the husbands were lovable buffoons. During the show there was always a problem that caused a small to large conflict between the husband and wife. The wife was usually the more even keeled practical thinking one of the two who always stood by her man waiting patiently for him to get himself out of the mess he got himself into. In the end, (thirty minutes later) there was love and laughter, and everyone lived happily ever after.

The other stream that flowed into my head and painted a picture of marriage was the real life relationships I saw of neighbors and my witness of my mom and my step-dad Claire. Starting from within my own household, I had my mother and Claire as my first and primary marriage model. Everything about this model was wrong as I interpreted it by the age of twelve. I knew what marriage was not, but not necessarily what it should be. I saw no positive example of marriage in the first inner shell or in shell number two being my friends. It just so happened that all of my close friends were raised by a single mother or had an alcoholic dad in the picture.

The next shell outside of my friends were neighbors that lived next door or in other adjacent buildings. This too was filled with single mothers or with alcohol impaired dads. The families that I saw and had contact with were families like mine that were generally broken and/or not whole. These were the models of family that I saw and learned from. The one or two homes that had a husband/wife marriage that seemed free from alcohol and probably normal, I had little to zero contact with because I had no interaction with their kid/s. Except for the three to four times that I remember going to my mothers brother and sisters house; my aunt and uncle, I never was ever really around a marriage.

By the time I would propose to Apple the best positive example that I had seen of the dynamics of marriage was that of the Cosby Show and the Huxtable family. Both husband and wife were successful, healthy minded and family oriented. I feel sorry for the children nowadays as they have shows like the Family Guy, the Simpsons and the plethora of other sitcoms that purposely undermine the institution of marriage and indoctrinate false and immoral views. Combine that with the curriculum the schools are teaching and you have a greater risk of a less joyful, peaceful and healthier marriage than my generation.

In spite of my exposure to negative examples I did have an idea or positive picture in my mind of what a marriage should be like between two people who were in love. The husband and wife would agree on moral issues and would share some interests and likes; as well as openly communicate their dreams and fears. I would later learn that it was very important that they share the same faith. Because Apple and I did not, this would be one of the larger items in our relationship that brought about our eventual divorce. And last but not least, we would have much laughter. Except for the moral issues and our children when they were born we had little of the other parts of the picture. I knew Apple would be a faithful wife and that she had no desire to drink alcohol or do drugs. I also knew she would be a hard worker and loving mother. These things I adored and wanted as a wife, and Apple did fulfill these.

At the same time I also knew that with the exception of those traits I have just listed, we had very little in common. I did not like it, but I accepted it. Through the love of God I looked at what she had and chose to ignore the qualities she didn't have. I had my shortcomings as well that made me less than perfect, but I say all of this to say we were not 'two peas in a pod'. After our wedding we spent a night in an expensive hotel in downtown Minneapolis and the next day went over my mother's house to watch television and visit. Instead of being filled with love and excitement I was sad. I was hit over the head with a ton of bricks. I am married to a woman whom I am not in love with. Two weeks later we moved into the house we purchased on 2416 Parkview Blvd in Golden Valley. A time that is supposed to be blissful and exciting before children are born was quiet and boring in our new home. Around three weeks after we moved into our new house, Apple hesitantly told me she thought she was pregnant. I did not jump up and down yelling with excitement nor did I curse and ask how did this happen. My response was somewhere in the middle. Our quiet life was going to change and I was excited about it.

After we had children there was a unique bond that developed that separated her from all of the other women in the world; she was the mother of my children. I had more reason to love her and make every effort for us to have a healthy and normal marriage. Our marriage was difficult for both of us because we were not completely meeting each others needs. I am not saying I was smarter than her because Apple was no dummy, but because she had limited knowledge of American history, no desire to speak about deeper philosophical ideas and no interest in Christianity, we had a shallow relationship. Apple was also more serious than I and this resulted in a lot less laughter than I wanted.

At the beginning of our relationship we went out dancing to a couple of clubs. Apple loved to dance and was a very good dancer. I on the other hand was becoming more and more uncomfortable with the environment of the night clubs. By the time we got married I had stopped going altogether and Apple would continue to go periodically with a friend. If you mixed in the occasional movie, going out to eat, and a visit to my moms house, that would be the full gamut of our fun time together.

Mom and Apple sharing a laugh.

There was an event in our early marriage that would set the parameters of our social life.

Apple and I were invited to an outing at a park with a couple of my friends and their families from work. It was a beautiful Saturday afternoon and I was looking forward to having a nice social visit. Apple would meet a couple of my new Christian friends from work and their wives and kids; and we would begin to develop friendships as a couple. We arrived with little Arias in tow and made the introductions. After awhile I went off with one of the men and thought it would be a good thing to leave her alone with the other women there. Apple was very anxious and uncomfortable and spoke very little. She used Arias as a distraction to wander away from the group and stayed isolated until I found her. We cut our stay short and went home. It was then that I realized we would not have many social group encounters because she felt very uncomfortable. She told me that she felt stupid and did not want to embarrass me. Apple spoke with an accent, but her English was very good. I told her that my friends and I do not and would not think that. So from that point on in our marriage until we would divorce, we had only a handful of social engagements. We generally only had people over our house on the kid's birthdays and when I went to a friend's house it was just the kids who went with me.

During this time I did have my old friend John who would come over quite often and we would play games in the late evening. I did not like this social limitation but I accepted it. In hindsight I look back and see how blessed I was because of this. Instead of going out and having good old fashion clean fun, I spent a lot of my free time studying the bible. My biblical understanding and spiritual growth was accelerated because of this.

With that said, our marriage eventually became nothing more than two ships passing in the night as we raised our two children.

CHAPTER 16

Barney and the Power Rangers

If I break down life into its components, marriage and fatherhood are head and shoulders above everything else in value and rewards. It was not until I became a father did I realize how powerful the emotion of love I would have for my children. All of the clichés regarding the love a parent has for their child began to resonate in my heart. Wanting the best for them and willing to sacrifice all for them is how I felt and continue to feel. I will make no pretensions that I was a perfect dad. I said and did things that were wrong and regrettable, and could have done many things better.

Life is like a videotape; once the event in time has happened you can only relive and experience the sweetness in memory and for me it's not enough. I miss the various stages in life and those precious simple moments of holding them when they were a baby or toddler. Reviewing memories in my head or watching old video recordings for me bring only sadness because I feel I could and should have given one more hug, been a little more patient, or told them how much I love them. The very old proverb is so true, and that is, you do not realize how important a person is until they are absent in your life. And if you realize it to late you will have lost out on life moments that can not be replicated. I say this to all of you moms and dads with little kids who are wearing you out. Enjoy them because they grow up very fast.

Exactly nine months to the day after Apple and I were married on June 30, 1989, Arias Anthani Oliver was born on April 1, 1990. But two months before this something quite heavenly had happened. *"Do not forget to entertain strangers, for by so doing some people have entertained angels without knowing it." (Heb 13:2)* When Apple was six to seven months pregnant with our first child, we received a visit from an old man who I believe was an angel. It was in the middle of winter Jan/Feb and I saw him walk up our street with no jacket on. It was not a very cold day, but have you ever seen a man in what appeared to be his 70s not wearing a jacket in the middle of the winter? I watched him walk into my driveway and then up the stairs from my big picture window in the living room. He knocked on the door and I went over and opened it. He said hello and asked for a glass of water. Apple who was in the living room with me went back to the kitchen to get him a glass of water as he waited outside. She returned with the glass of water and gave it to him to drink. He said thank you, but before he left he told Apple not to worry and that her baby was going to be alright.

Apple took the glass from him and walked back to the kitchen to put it in the sink. She walked back out into the living room which would have only been about twenty to thirty seconds and went to the picture window to look for the old man. She didn't see him so she went outside and walked down the steps to the street. She looked both ways and saw nobody. How could an old man just disappear? And why would he walk in the middle of the winter without a jacket and go up to our house for a glass of water? The answer is God loved Apple. Apple never told me until after this encounter but she had been worrying very much about her pregnancy. After the old man left or who I believe was an angel left, Apple's pregnancy anxieties went away.

It was a little past midnight when he was born and I was in for quite the April fool's joke. After the doctor gave Arias a spank on his little butt and showed Apple her new son, they took Arias away to clean him up before placing him into a warm baby incubator. Mom and I went in to see him and everyone including mom was gushing about how beautiful he was. I on the other hand was missing the beauty of his beautiful brown eyes, head full of hair and instead stared at his football shaped head. My poor son I thought would have a life ahead of him that would be filled with people gawking at him and even calling him names. How was I going to protect him and help him have a happy life? I kept asking myself why no one was verbalizing the obvious deformity.

After a few minutes of silence my mother asked me if I was alright. I told her what I was thinking and then she laughed and set me straight. It reminded me of the original Saturday Night Live program in the late 1970s that had a popular skit called the Coneheads. They were a family from outer space who had giant football shaped cone heads. To counter the potential alienation (pun) they would have received because of their huge football shaped craniums, they told everyone they were from the country of France. Arias Oliver who was born in America, whose father is an American and his mother is a Thailandeese, is none of the above but is a Frenchman. I wonder if I was the only father in the world who did not know that all babies have French heads when they are delivered normally. April Fools Wade!

Finally, victory over drugs!

Apple was extremely instrumental in helping me quit a deeply engrained bad habit, but she was not the all in all. While we were dating she mentioned nothing about my marijuana usage. A few months after we were married she caught me smoking in the garage. She had been telling me not to long after we were married that she did not want me to smoke anymore. I told her I would quit. We walked upstairs into the living room arguing and before you know it this 110 lb woman turned into the Incredible Hulk. She threatened me and said she would not tolerate me smoking. She picked up a lamp and hurled it at me. She did not want the father of her child to be a druggie. I knew she was right and I loved her for taking a stand, but all she did was slow me down. That was all part of God's plan and in the June 1990 timeframe He would choose to use one more thing and it was the most precious and innocent thing in my life.

The final surgical tool, cleansing agent, mountain mover, and piece of the puzzle that God would use to give me victory over drugs would be my two month old son Arias. Apple had an opportunity to get out of the house and rejuvenate with a friend, so it was my little boy and I home alone on a Saturday night. The television was on, all of the lights were on and the two of us were in the living room. I smoked some weed and was feeling good. After getting high I picked up Arias and held him in my lap as I sat in the chair in the dining room. I positioned him so we were looking at each other. I was enjoying and admiring my boy. Arias with his beautiful eyes, was staring at my eyes and then I began to cry. His eyes peered into my heart and said "dad why are you doing this, don't you love me? You hated that Claire was an alcoholic and said you would never be like him, but you are like him. Your drug of choice is weed not alcohol, but it is really the same. I am ashamed of you as a father, my dad is a loser."

I was looking at my two month old son sobbing and feeling this overwhelming flood of shame. I stopped looking into his eyes because I could not stand the pain. I told Arias I was sorry and that I would quit because I loved him so much. I wanted to be the father to him that I never had. That was arguably the most life changing night in my life. God had used my baby boy to get me over the last hurdle and cross the finish line of a drug free life. My greatest hearts desire was to be a great father and now it would be possible.

In order to rid myself of the addiction and develop a new life style of sobriety, I had to make a couple of changes. I cut the string on all relationships with people who used and kept myself away from gatherings or businesses that catered to drinking. For the next five years I would be completely clean and had zero desire to smoke. Never in my life did I think I would be drug free. I said completely clean for five years, because I had a relapse where I smoked on three occasions in a two week window five years later. On the third and final time I had a scare that closed the door permanently on marijuana. I had closed my eyes to go to sleep still a little high from smoking. As soon as I closed my eyes I saw two very evil eyes staring at me. I opened my eyes and they were gone. When I closed them again they appeared again. I cried out to God for help.

The bible condemns the practice of sorcery and all people who practiced it were cut off from God. The Greek word for sorcery is *pharmakia*. This was the language of the original manuscripts of our current day bible. The English equivalent of *pharmakia* is pharmacy. In sorcery the use of drugs, whether simple or potent, was generally accompanied by incantations and appeal to occult powers. The Native American Indians practice this as do various voodoo practitioners in Africa, Haiti and other places throughout the world.

God condemned this because the spirits behind this are demons and the use of drugs is a gateway for demons into the spirit of man. The history books and police ledgers are full of people who have done horrific things because they took drugs and said they were involuntarily under the control, or could not resist the pressure from another being that spoke to them inside of their head. I told God that I understood what was happening. His patience has a limit, and if I choose to use after this time, I will risk great harm to my self. He will allow more than these demon eyes to scare me. I told God to please forgive me and that I would never do it again and the eyes disappeared. That was the last time I ever smoked pot.

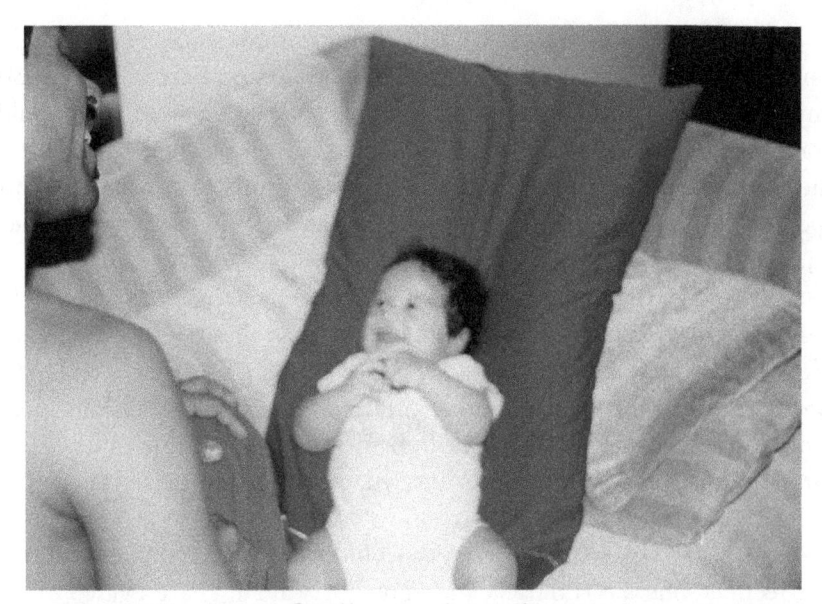

The inspiration to finally stop doing drugs, my son Arias.

Six months after Arias was born I talked Apple into having another child. I wanted two kids and I wanted them close in age. I always felt that the three year difference between Cory and me was a significant factor that prevented us from having a healthy relationship. I did not want that factor in play with my kids. So on August 15, 1991 God gave us a beautiful and healthy baby girl. We named her Ajaa Abyana Oliver. There was no cone head shock this time because Ajaa was born through a caesarean section. I may have initially wanted another son but when she was born I realized that it was now perfect. I had a son and daughter and now felt complete. Two months later I went to the doctor and he performed surgery on me so that my gun would only shoot blanks. I joke that I was trying to think about the weather and the professional baseball team the Twins, because the doctor's assistant was an attractive lady my age. It bordered on cruel and unusual treatment.

After the birth of Arias and Ajaa, my next great memory was that of Arias when he was around seven months old. I got off work and went home after working the graveyard shift. As I was walking up the steps to the door there was my little man holding on to the ledge of the giant picture window smiling and waiting for me. Before he was able to walk he would hear my car roll into the driveway and he would crawl over and prop himself up. When I walked into the house Arias would have a smile as big as the sun, and say "da-de, da-de". Every problem I had or thought I had, vanished and was replaced with pure joy. At no time in my life was any human being ever that excited to see me. When his sister Ajaa would come into the world fifteen months later the both of them would greet me every morning they were awake with the attitude that I was the most special person in the world. My heart would melt. Now it is only "hey dad".

I should have named Arias, Mocha Java. Not because he had a light coffee complexion but because he was as hyper as a double shot of espresso. He is twenty now and is still as hyper as he was then. From the moment he was born I read the bible and other children's books to him. We wrestled around on the carpet and I took him to visit his grandma quite often. Grandma Oliver was on cloud nine when he was born and the two of them quickly developed a bond.

If Arias was like coffee, then Ajaa would have been compared to a lazy boy recliner. She was laid back, and in no hurry at all. I have a video where I am sitting on the floor watching television changing Ajaa's diaper and Arias is badgering me asking if I am done so he can play with her. As soon as I am done sliding her pants over her diaper, Arias grabs her by both of her feet and starts pulling her around the living room. Mr. Mocha Java was pulling lazy girl around like a toy and the both of them were having fun.

A few months later I walked out of the bathroom and Ajaa was Casper the ghost with two brown eyes. Arias had poured a container of baby powder all over her head. He would then tap her head and watch the cloud of powder explode. Mr. Mocha Java was at it again and Ms. Recliner was just chillin. My immediate reaction was laughter, but then I scolded Arias and told him that he was wrong for doing that and he needed to stop tapping her head. Ajaa saw that I was angry so she started to cry, but Arias must have thought I was talking to another person named Arias and continued with his head pat explosions. It is hard to be taken serious by a two year old when you are laughing. We did not have any more baby powder escapades but the pattern of Ajaa being the lady in the box and Arias being the magician with the saw would continue without ceasing up to the present.

We were fortunate that we did not have a need for child daycare. I worked nights and Apple worked part-time in the Afternoons. I would arrive home around 6:30 am and jump into bed and sleep for 6 ½ hours. Apple would wake up with the kids and take care of them until I got out of bed. Every day at exactly 1:00 pm, plus or minus two to three seconds, the bedroom door would crash open and both of them would storm into the bedroom screaming "get up da-de", as they climbed onto the waterbed. It was as violent a way to wake up as anyone could imagine. You had two bubbly very loud and happy toddlers bouncing on the bed speaking in their outside voices telling me to wake up. Apple's shift had ended and she did not work overtime.

After slowly crawling out of bed, I would enter the land of the living and turn into Superdad until I went to work at 9:00 pm. I can say that because the kids thought I was a superhero. I was their best friend, protector, provider, entertainer, teacher, and helper. As the years went by, my superhero status diminished, then faded away entirely when they became teen agers. Once I came into the living room, Apple would metaphorically jump off the top rope in the wrestling ring and tag my hand to come into the ring. It would be my turn to wrestle the two smalls and she would have a breather for the rest of the day until she had to go to work in the mid afternoon. She only worked part-time and on the days she didn't have to go to work it meant some of those days I had an opportunity to go to the park and play basketball for about an hour and a half.

A typical day in the life of Superdad included walking up to the park, reading books including illustrated bible stories, playing in the house, being the safety monitor, spoon feeding the baby food or meal that Apple had made for dinner, diaper changing and pajama time. I would wake up at 1:00 and by the time 4:00 in the afternoon rolled around I was beat. Thank God for Barney and the Power Rangers. For a whole hour I could lie on the couch and take a cat nap because they were both plopped in front of the television absorbed with the purple dinosaur and the four young super hero's who beat up monsters. I personally enjoyed both shows myself and I am not ashamed to say that Barney rocks. As soon as my babysitting friends on television left I rolled off the couch went into the phone booth and came out and resumed the role of Superdad until Apple came home from work, which was a little before I had to leave to go to work. Except for the weekends I was with the kids all by my self most of the time when I was awake.

I did have one weekend without the kids in the first five years of being a dad. Apple took both Arias and Ajaa up with Mike V. to visit his mom up north in Brainerd. They left on Friday afternoon and were scheduled to come home in the afternoon on Sunday. I had to work Friday evening and then take advantage of getting a full eight hours of sleep when I got home. Saturday came and went very quick, but I was excited that I would be able to wake up around 9:00 Sunday morning and have a nice quiet five to six hours of solitude before Apple brought the kids back home. It never happened. I was still in bed when around 8:30 the circus (primarily Arias) came back home. My one and only weekend by my self never really materialized. I was mad but somehow did not say anything.

Since Arias almost never took a nap and was always on the move, Apple and I were generally fatigued. It was not until five years later that I learned we should have scheduled a nap and specific bedtime for both of them. It would have been beneficial for them and given Apple and me a breather during the day. Because we didn't, Arias was generally on the move like the Energizer bunny starting at 6:00 am until 9:30 pm with Ajaa quietly tagging along.

My first five years of being a father were physically and emotionally exhausting. One would have thought that running on half empty would have prevented me from learning anything but that was not the case. During this time of my life as I was growing in my faith, I began to understand God in a deeper way because I was a father. The bible says he is our Father and since I really did not have a father, this relational term was a little hollow to me. While being a father I began to do fatherly things and experience deep emotions for Arias and Ajaa that are ascribed to God in the bible. I wanted to give gifts which Apple and I were able to do on birthdays, Christmas, and throughout the year, with the biggest gift being my self. I wanted them to be safe, so I put boundaries up in their lives and watched. If they were close to trouble and I had an opportunity, I would jump in to save. If they did get hurt I tried to turn life's bumps in the road into a learning lesson to make them a better person. These are just a couple of examples that apply to God in a deeper and more dynamic way.

But most importantly, I found out that there was nothing in the world that Arias and Ajaa could do that would make me stop loving them. I began to feel and act from the same emotions that God has for me. My heart would be sad when they got hurt or were sad, and would rejoice when they were rejoicing. When I understood my fatherly feelings were a dimmer carbon copy to what the bible says about God who feels the same way to those who have embraced his son Jesus, my relationship with God went to another level. *"For I am convinced that neither death, nor life, neither angels nor demons, neither the present nor the future, nor any powers, neither height nor depth, nor anything else in al creation, will be able to separate us from the love of God that is in Christ Jesus our Lord". (Rom 8:38-39)*

I remember an old Flintstones cartoon I watched back when I was a kid. Fred was a proud papa so he took out his movie camera and filmed his little baby girl Pebbles doing everything including eating, sleeping, and everything else that was monotonously common. He invited his best buddy and his wife over (Barney and Betty Rubble), to watch his new home movies. To make this long story short, they all got bored very quickly and wanted to leave. With that I will end this with two events that happened with little Arias and Ajaa.

This first incident is really classified more in the astonishing description than anything else. If this is actually normal animal behavior and most people have seen this when they go to the zoo, then I need to start watching more wildlife programs on television. We have two zoos in Minnesota, the older, smaller and free Como Park and the more modern, larger and pay to get in zoo called 'The New Zoo'. On this occasion I took the kids to the 'empty daddy's pocket book' zoo. Arias, Ajaa and I began our day meandering through the inside part where birds and smaller animals were housed. I was pushing Ajaa in the baby stroller and Arias was out in front walking. It was great watching Arias get excited about some of the animals, whereas Ajaa was a little to young to appreciate.

After walking through some of the animal exhibits we came upon a solitary monkey in a fenced in enclosure. I do not remember what kind of monkey it was but it was perched sitting about twenty feet in the air on one of the limbs in a tree. Arias looked at the monkey and with his one second attention span began to proceed to the next exhibit. Remember Mr. Mocha Java was a mover. As I gazed up and looked at the monkey, the monkey leered at me with a very angry look and then held out his hand and gave me the middle finger. I could not believe it. As long as I stared he held it up. I told the monkey that what he was doing was not very nice and I laughed. I starting walking away and after a few steps I stopped and looked back up at the monkey. He was staring at me and as soon as I stopped, he lifted up his hand and gave me the middle finger again. Thank God the rest of the animals at the zoo that day did not show me contempt like that primate did. If they did I may have developed an anti Dr. Doolittle complex.

P.S. little monkey buddy, I know why you were alone in the cage. You are a jerk. (If you want to know what my take on this is, read Mark 5:13).

If you are feeling like Barney and Betty, please don't go yet. This last story is something all parents can relate to.

It is true that all parents think about the sound of silence when their kid/s are making a joyful noise. But as soon as it the noise ends and it is quiet our internal 'trouble radar' starts to beep. Arias was four years old and Ajaa was two years old when the three of us went up to the grocery store to do a little shopping. It is very clever of stores to put smaller things that you really don't need and had no desire to purchase up by the cash register. While waiting you take in all of these temptations and then conclude your life would be a little better if you had one of those items. Many people fall prey to that temptation and on this occasion Arias and Ajaa would become caught in the trap. Take a kid grocery shopping and inevitably they will see something they want and will ask for it. On this occasion while the three of us were waiting in the check out line, Arias asked if he could have this candy item. I told him "no" and that he needed to put it back. I do not remember but if Arias held to form he would have asked again and I would have told him "no" again. I paid the cashier for whatever I came to get and then the three of us went home.

I do not remember what I was doing but about fifteen minutes after arriving home I noticed that there was no noise. Since I did not lose my sense of hearing and Arias did not know how to be quiet, I knew something was wrong so I began to investigate. After putting on my Magnum P.I. multicolored Hawaiian shirt and using my Sherlock Holmes magnifying glass, I tracked them down and found them sitting in their closet. They were leaning up against the back of the wall eating the loot they had extracted from the grocery store via the 'five finger discount'. They were busted. They knew they had done something wrong and that is why they were hiding in their closet.

I told them I was very disappointed and what they did was very wrong. I told them I was going to take them to the police station and that the police were going to put them in jail. I put them in the car and drove to the police station. At the police station a policeman told Arias and Ajaa that he wouldn't put them in jail if they promised not to steal again. They both agreed and we all went home. This may qualify as the youngest age group that has ever been 'Scared Straight' in the United States of America. So I am proud to say that my little Bonnie & Clyde retired and became givers instead of takers.

CHAPTER 17

Delana and the Demon

Very soon after Arias was born a person from the past resurfaced in our lives and needed a place to live for a little while. After Apple had moved out of her stepdad Mike's house and into my apartment, her friend Delana continued to stay at Mike's not making any attempt to find another place. After a couple of weeks Mike told Delana that she had to find another place to live. A few weeks later she moved out and moved in with some people in the Lake St. area of Minneapolis. There may have been a few phone calls at the beginning but after time Delana dropped off the radar. About a year later she contacted Apple and said she had joined the Army. She had no where to go and the Armed Forces of America gave her an opportunity to make something of herself.

To our surprise Delana made it through all of the entrance exams and tests and was cleared to go to basic training. Apple and I were happy for her but in the back of our mind we thought she was not going to make it. She was a chain smoker who did not have a strong work ethic or even a middle of the road work ethic. About four weeks into her basic training we got a call from the Army base confirming our apprehensions. She was having some really big problems that they did not go into detail with and asked us some questions. Delana must have given them our number as a contact. So after four weeks she was discharged from the US ARMY and sent home from basic training.

Before she left Delana asked Apple who in turned asked me if she could stay with us for a little while until she found a job. I knew Delana had no family to help her or any good friends, so we said yes. Delana moved in and had the second bedroom of the house for herself. In the other bedroom it was Apple, me and our little baby boy Arias.

Delana grew up and lived in a real life horror movie. Instead of being nurtured, protected and loved, Delana was repeatedly sexually molested by her monster of a father, and was even forced to watch porn movies with him. Delana opened up her heart to Apple and shared her life story after an incident that took place on a Metro Transit Bus they were riding together on. They were traveling somewhere in South Minneapolis when a man boarded the bus. As soon as Delana saw this man she ran off the bus screaming hysterically. It was her father. Delana had run away from home sometime in her middle teens and this was the first time she saw him in years. All of those suppressed memories that were locked up in the video vault of her brain were released and as a deer instinctively runs away from a wolf so too did she. Apple got off of the bus and ran after her.

If the abuse and neglect she received from her father was not enough for a young girl to deal with, her mother had serious mental problems that placed her in one of Minnesota's state mental hospitals. I know this because when I would later have to remove Delana from our house, I went through all of her belongings looking for anything dangerous as well as any information that could possible help her get help. I came across medical/legal records that stated Delana and her mother suffered from a bi-polar mental condition. It did not say what any of the behavioral problems were, but my guess is she was like Delana. Between the mother's bi-polar mental condition and her evil father, Delana developed multiple personalities. If you have seen the 1970s movie Sybil, Delana was like that.

I remember when it was aired on television in 1976 or 1977. Mom told me that I should not watch it because I might get scared. I watched it anyway and it freaked me out. After the movie I went to bed but I could not sleep. I got out of bed and went to my mom's bedroom. I can't remember what she said to comfort me, but it ended with me turning on the lights in the hallway and laying outside of her bedroom door. I was spooked like I have never been before.

One of the stories Apple had told me about Delana was the time when she changed into one of her other personalities while they were driving to Brooklyn Center shopping mall. Out of the blue while Delana was sitting in the passenger seat, she began to talk like a boy of about eight years of age. Apple thought it was strange and was a little unnerved but for whatever reason said she wasn't spooked. I on the other hand probably would have had heart failure, lost control of the car and driven into oncoming traffic.

Inside of the mall and at one of the stores Apple had purchased something and was waiting for Delana in front of the store entrance. Delana and/or one her inner persons had stolen something and she was stopped by a store clerk or security person. Apple saw the confrontation and Delana crying so she walked over to see what was going on. The security person looked very confused because Delana was talking and sobbing like a little boy. Delana said she did not understand what was going on. After Delana surrendered the item to the security person, he let her go. On the way home she continued crying saying she did not understand what happened.

Apple told me about this along time before she had even went into the army. I never saw Delana act any different than herself on any of the occasions we were together, so I did not have any fears that she would be a danger to me, Apple, or Arias. Two weeks after she moved in with us after getting discharged from the Army, Delana went out on the deep end and told Apple on a night I was at work that she wanted to burn Arias in the fireplace. Apple went in her room, locked the bedroom door and slept with one eye on the door and the other on Arias. As soon as I came home from work that Saturday morning Apple told me what Delana has said.

I let Delana sleep and when she woke up I told her I wanted to talk to her. The two of us sat across the dining room table from each other and I told her what Apple had said. I also told her that I knew about her multiple personalities. I was a young baby Christian who knew that I was dealing with demonic possession but was not sure on how I was to deal with this situation. I told her because she wanted to roast Arias in the fireplace that she had to move out immediately today. I began to explain to her that the first and foremost pressing issue was her need for divine intervention. I shared with her how much Jesus loves her and that he wants to help her.

As soon as I started talking about Jesus, Delana began to talk in a very masculine and low voice. She or actually (he) said that he was from Africa. He knew who Jesus was and has seen him. I became mesmerized by what I was seeing and hearing. I prodded her (him) about Jesus and then her eyes changed and became the most evil filled scary eyes I have ever seen. She/he began speaking in a foreign language and I leaned back and got up out of my chair and walked backwards into the kitchen where Apple and Arias were. I was very scared and did not know what I should do. I thought of the demon possessed men in the Gospels who were very violent and had superhuman strength so that they could not be restrained. I was thinking Wade, you really blew it now.

After I got up Delana walked into the bathroom and locked the door. She was in their babbling really loud in a language that was indiscernible to me. A couple of months prior I had been invited by a sweet lady at work, Loretta, to a Saturday night bible study. It was there that I met Ms Dorothy B. She was a long time follower of Jesus and I knew she would be able to help me. I called her up on the telephone and told her what was going on. Dorothy began to pray over the phone and after a few minutes Delana came out of the bathroom calmed down. Whether Delana was Delana at that time I do not know, but she was not that evil demon speaking that foreign language. I can't remember what I said to her but I convinced her to take a ride with Apple and me to go get something to eat. She agreed and the four of us got into the car and drove off. Apple and Arias were in the backseat. When I looked back at Apple she was in a state of shock. She didn't say a word the whole time she was in the car. I had no clue where I was going but my plan was to drop Delana off somewhere faraway. After getting Delana safely removed from the house I would then figure out where and when to deliver her few possessions.

As I was driving, Delana turned into this woman speaking in a very, very, very sensual voice. She was touching me and telling me that we should drop off Apple so the two of us could be together. She said she hated Apple and loved me. I told her that was a great idea. I looked in the backseat and I could see the gears in Apple's head were spinning. I was driving around not knowing where I should go and how I would get her out of the car. I pulled over on Washington Ave in the Seven Corners area by Highway 35W and told Delana to get out and put a couple coins in the parking meter so we could go into the restaurant to eat. She did not trust me so she waited until I got out of the car before she got out her self. As soon as she got out and stepped away from the car, I told Apple to lock the door. Apple did and I ran around to my side and jumped in. Delana walked over to the car and with a frozen stare of diabolical contempt peered at Apple.

I pulled away from the curb, took a right at the corner so I could turn around and go back home. After turning around I came back to the corner with the stop light. Delana had crossed the street and was standing on the corner by the passenger side. She looked like a frozen statue. She did not blink and was staring at me with hatred. This wave of compassion fell over me and I unlocked the door and let her get back in. I drove back home and I called the police. The police came out and I told them what was going on. They interviewed Delana and she denied everything.

The police told her that they were going to bring her down to Hennepin County Medical Center for an evaluation. She did not want to go but they took her anyway. She was admitted into the Psych Ward and stayed there about a week. They called about six days later and told Apple and me that they could not hold her any longer. Sometime after Delana was discharged she came over to get the few clothes and possessions she had. She had found some small apartment in Minneapolis. Apple, Delana and I drove to her apartment and dropped her and her possessions off. The only possessions she had were a couple suitcases of clothes, an alarm radio and a small television we gave her. I felt very sorry for her.

I am fuzzy on the date but about a month later Apple had called me at work for the first time in our marriage. It was relayed to me that I was to call home immediately. I called home and Apple was very nervous. Delana had showed up at the front door with a couple of shady characters and wanted to come in. Delana knew I worked nights and that Apple was home alone with the baby. Apple talked through the door and said no. Delana became angry and said she was going to do something bad to Apple. I told Apple to call the police, but Apple said since Delana had left she didn't feel she needed to.

I left work to go patrol around my block hoping to find Delana in the area but she was nowhere to be seen. I went into the house to see how Apple was. She was anxious and would be for the next week. The next night I went to work at the usual time but left work about a half hour later. I parked on the street behind our house and crept through our neighbor's yard, over his fence and into my backyard. I hid behind a tree looking and waiting for them to come back. After about 10 minutes I went inside to see how Apple was doing. I made sure the house was secure and then I went back to work. Besides my self, I had asked a few believers at work to pray for Apple and Arias' safety. God answered our prayer and Delana showed up only one more time but never got out of the car. A few months had passed without a peep from Delana when I came across her obituary in the Sunday newspaper. She had died at the age of twenty-four.

CHAPTER 18

Divorce and Remarriage

In 1993 my marriage started to sprout leaks. At the end of 1994 the holes became larger and the bitter waters of life began to flow through more and more, slowly flooding our future together. It started out great on New Year's 1995. We went to the casino and she watched me win a small amount of money at the black jack table. We had gone to the casino one or two other times before that. The month of January came and went and we seemed to be enjoying each other and heading in the right direction. Before New Years we had been quarrelling quite a bit for a long period of time. Divorce had been brought up but now it was a thing of the past.

As the year moved along, Apple began to work more hours in her new job as a nursing assistant. We began to see less and less of each other. On our wedding anniversary I had bought her some flowers and made plans for us to go out to eat and have a romantic evening. She was happy to receive the flowers but said she had already made plans to go out dancing with her friend. I became livid. All of my pent up resentments in the past year was released and I told her if you don't love me than let's get a divorce. She said O.K. She had called my bluff and in my pride I said, "that is what we will do".

I looked in the paper under divorce and found an advertisement that said divorce's for $100 if there were no contentions. I told Apple that I wanted the kids. She said no way, and I said "I will never let you take them from me." Apple said the same thing and then started crying. It was unquestionable the lowest and saddest day in our marriage. I never told Apple, but it grieved me terribly to see her crying. What can be uglier than a husband and wife threatening each other with taking their precious children away from the other? A few weeks later Apple told me she thought it was best for Arias and Ajaa if they lived with me in our house. I reassured Apple that there would be no visitation restrictions for her and the kids. With that, a few months later she moved into her own apartment.

During this time, my mother would come over the house at night to watch Arias and Ajaa, and stay until I would wake in the early afternoon. It was a physical hardship for my mother who had poor health but she did it and I was and will be forever grateful. Without her help I do not know how I would have been able to manage. All throughout this time while Apple was gone, I was wrestling with anger. She had left the kids and me and had created a stressful situation for my mother and me. I was still hopeful and spent time at home and at work with my Christian brothers praying for reconciliation. God heard my prayer but answered it differently than what I was asking for. He had a plan for Apple, Arias, Ajaa and me and it did not include a divorce reprieve. He honored Apple's wish to leave and on November 30, 1995 we were officially divorced. It was a sad day. Whatever my 'at fault' percentage was, did not matter, I had failed.

In August/September of 1997, I spoke with Apple on the phone. After our divorce she had become increasingly bitter towards me. She was different this time. Instead of her usual indignant tone she had with me, she was talking in a peaceful spirit. She told me that she had been watching television and had come to a channel that was broadcasting a Billy Graham crusade. She said she wanted to change it because she did not want to be reminded of me preaching to her when we were married. Due to forces outside of her control she was not able to change the channel and continued to watch the program. At the end of the program Billy Graham gave an invitation to the people there in person and those who were watching on television. Almost twenty years before, the young girl who sat on the railroad tracks in Thailand and wondered if there was a God, had finally stopped wondering. Jesus had been knocking on the door of her heart for many years and Apple had finally opened the door and invited him in.

Horribly, a month afterward, Apple would be diagnosed with stomach cancer and die nine months later. It was very hard to watch her slowly die. She did not want to die and fought as hard and as long as any person who has ever lived. She loved Arias and Ajaa very much and did not want to leave them. At the funeral, one of her co-workers who happened to be a Christian read the eulogy. I have been to a few funerals and I may be a little biased, but I believe the eulogy that was read was one of the best ever. It was a beautiful description of a life changed by God in a very short period of time. Someone other than the writer who was unable to attend read the eulogy. So you do not get confused, Apple's birth and legal name was Rome. Here is the eulogy dated July 25, 1998.

"The last time that I visited with Rome, she asked if I would write her eulogy for her. I agreed, but have to admit that I put it off as long as possible hoping for some last minute miracle. Since Rome's diagnosis, a lot of people that I know began to think about life a little bit more than usual and about just how short that our life on earth really is. Unfortunately, in this me, me, me world, it almost always takes a tragedy or the death of someone so young to make us think of the existence of God and whether or not there is a heaven and a hell. I met Rome at the time in her life when God was drawing her near to him. We used to go on break together at work and she always had so many questions about God and what she had to do to become clean before God. We did a lot of studying and reading, but since I live so far away, beyond study at work, she was pretty much on her own to find God and his will for her life.

Rome changed so much in such a short period of time. In years past, Rome had had quite a foul mouth. Because of God in her life, she gave this up because she realized that it was wrong. She gave away clothes that she felt were too 'racy' or tight on her because she felt that God did not approve of her wearing them anymore. In past situations at work where she might have mouthed off or gotten mad and confronted the offending party, she backed down and forgave without incident at all. I personally know how much it took for her to do that!!

She wanted to go back to school so bad, and yet every time she tried to get there, some obstacle was always in her way. She resolved to herself that if God wanted her to go back to school, he would make the way and it would be in his timing. All these changes in Rome's life were not because she was a saint or because she considered herself better than anyone else, it was God working in her life, plain and simple, end of story. It made me so happy to see that God had taken her under his wing as his child. She gave up the ways that had once made her happy and yielded to God and his ways for her life to make him happy. It was shortly after these changes began, that the earth shattering diagnosis of cancer came into play. It is hard for a person who has walked close with God for many years to take that kind of news, so imagine how a young Christian such as Rome must have felt!!

There were so many people devastated at Rome's prognosis!! It became very apparent after Rome's first surgery that she had made an impact on so many people at Methodist Hospital besides me. We started a collection at work for Rome with the hope of raising $1000.00. In my wildest dreams, I could not have imagined the response we got. We ended up raising enough money for three months rent and utilities, three months worth of car payments, and enough money to buy her children presents for Christmas. God was so good to her in her final months!!

The initial diagnosis was hard on Rome, but after the first surgery, I never heard her cry or complain once. Last week when we were together, the worst that came out of her mouth was, "this sucks…I want to eat and I can't". I had to agree… it did suck. She was young, she wanted to see her kids graduate and get married; she wanted to live.

The conversation that came out of her statement was this, it was better for her to be dying at 32 and going to heaven, than to be 95 and dying and going to hell. That is the peace of God in her life and in her heart, and none of us could have given it to her, and none of us could have taken it away. She faced death by holding onto God's hand and trusting in him. He didn't give her the reason for her illness, he simply asked her to trust, and she did.

Well, between God, Rome, and me, we make her eulogy a lesson, hopefully a lesson that will help someone else somewhere along the line. Rome was told by one so-called Christian that her cancer was a punishment from God for the life that she had previously lived. First of all, unless we know God's thoughts and he has told us that her cancer is a punishment, we walk on dangerous ground putting words in his mouth. I know this was an issue that Rome wanted addressed. Secondly, my own input into the issue is this, God loves everyone. He may not like the things we do, but he does love us. He shows it everyday. Knowing that he is our heavenly father, and he has also made me a parent myself, this is what I will share with you from what I know of him.

First of all, we're all going to die. We may be young, we may be old, we may be sick for a long time or it may be very sudden, but none of us here will escape it. If cancer really is a punishment form God, then each one of us in this room should have it right now. There has never been one person on this earth besides God himself, manifested in Jesus Christ, who has lived a sinless life. No sin is greater than any other in God's eyes, you've either sinned or you haven't, and every one of us has. Rome had already had all the punishment from this world she could take and that is why she started seeking God in the first place. God had allowed all of the hurt and pain to take place in her life to bring her to a place that would guarantee her an eternal home in heaven. She became a Christian before her cancer came and I know that God did not punish her for becoming a Christian. Her cancer and death are no punishment at all because in death she has found paradise. I am jealous!! Imagine paradise and perfection, no more sickness, winter, pain, and disappointment forever and ever and ever. Forever never ends and that is a long time". There was a little bit more but I have chosen to exclude it. What this all means to me is that Apple is with God and I, Arias and Ajaa will one day see her again.

Throughout my marriage with Apple I would see married couples who had great communication, laughed together, prayed together, worked on problems together and had fun together. Because the quantity and quality of those things were in short supply in my marriage, I would periodically get depressed. Sometimes I would daydream about what it would be like to be married to a woman who offered that. I never thought it would actually happen to me. A week or two after my divorce with Apple I had given Vonda a call and asked if she would be willing to have a date with me that involved her six year old son Rico who I had never met, five year old Arias, four year old Ajaa and a mutual friend named Paula Goldstein and my mom. She agreed and on Saturday Dec 16th we would have our first date. She came over and we made homemade Christmas cards. The mood was festive and Cupid was shooting a lot of arrows. I was filled with a new source of refreshment as I would steal looks at this beautiful woman who was engaging in conversation and enjoyed making Christmas cards that were not generic but were boldly saying "Jesus is the reason for the season." The night ended and I walked her to her car and shook her hand. It would be the beginning of an everyday phone courtship that had us talking about marriage weeks later.

If you were wondering how I knew Vonda before I called her, I will tell you. During the stormy weather of my marriage my mother who gave up all hope, thought I should meet this young lady she thought would be a wonderful wife and mother for the kids and me. Mom had told me about her but I said that I am married and have no desire other than saving my marriage. I told her straight out that I did not want to meet her. Weeks later I had a doctor's appointment and I asked mom if she would watch Arias and Ajaa for a little bit. She said yes, so I drove over and dropped them off. As soon as I walked in I saw Vonda. Vonda would tell me later that she was spoon fed on a regular basis by my mom and a client/friend named Paula about how wonderful I was and that she too had to meet me. On this occasion she later caved in and went over my mom's house.

I walked in, saw Vonda, put on my smiley face and said hello. Inwardly the furnace kicked in and began to stoke the emotion of anger raising it close to a nuclear meltdown. I avoided any small talk and quickly got out of there. I never saw her or spoke with her again until I had called her for the date. I will let God be the judge as to how long I should have waited to call another woman for a date, but I find no shame in saying I was a lonely man who dreamed of having a wife/friend. I also had full custody of Arias and Ajaa and it was quite a burden I had put on my mother's shoulders as she stepped in to babysit Arias and Ajaa everyday that I worked. Well, long story short, we fell in love and were married five months later on April 27, 1996.

The beginning of a new and wonderful life.

Vonda was raised in a loving home by William and Joanne Mathena. They are great people filled with a lot of love who opened up their arms and adopted her when she was six months old. They have also been wonderful in-laws to me. Vonda and I love them very much and I want to say thank you for all that you have done for me individually and collectively as a family. I say that to preface the preceding paragraphs and so that I do not accidently hurt anyone.

I do not know how common it is that a mother or father will choose to not want to see their own child, but as with me and my father, Vonda would have her rejection magnified even more with the freakish behavior of her biological mother. When Vonda was twenty she contacted the adoption agency, filled out the necessary paperwork and submitted it with the hope that her biological mother would want to meet the daughter that she gave up for adoption. Not that she felt unloved by her mother and father, but she just had a little hole in her soul that wanted to know more about who she was by where she came from. Weeks later she received a reply from the agency that her mother agreed to meet her. The agency acted as a "go between" and set up a date for them to meet at the Applebee's restaurant on Lake St in the Lake Calhoun area.

Vonda was excited and went with guarded optimism. What happened next was something out of the Twilight Zone. Before I say what happened, lets write what one would logically presume would happen. The mother sees Vonda, walks over to her, says hello, they embrace, they both sob a little or a lot, and then they walk over to the table to sit, eat and talk. In their conversation the mother apologizes, says why she did what she did and they share each others life story. The mother says that she has off and on through the years thought of her and wondered how she was doing and says she can't believe they are sitting together. They end the meal with a smile and hug as they swap phone numbers so they can stay in touch. Vonda walks out of the restaurant with a smile and cherry pie all over her shirt but she doesn't care; life is good.

That sounded great and should have happened but the world we live in is broken and does not always end in fairy tale fashion. What really happened was just the opposite. The restaurant had not yet opened, so Vonda was waiting outside when her mother arrived. Vonda walked up to her and her mother looked at Vonda and said "I do not know why after all of these years you want to open this up." Instead of waiting for the restaurant to open they decided to walk around Lake Calhoun and talk. Vonda said she mostly listened as her mother complained about her life. After walking awhile they turned around and went back to the restaurant to get some lunch. One of the things Vonda asked Joan about was her father. Joan replied "be glad you do not know who he is."

After lunch, Joan said "the least she could do was pay for the meal," and she did. As they were in the parking lot heading for their cars, Joan told Vonda that she had a half brother and sister who were a couple years younger than her. Vonda was born in 1969. She shook Vonda's hand and said, "please do not ever contact me again." Vonda got into her car and quietly drove away.

The real tragedy is that she has a younger brother and sister who do not know she exists. Vonda tried a few years ago through the adoption agency to find out who her brother and sister are, but Joan had put a block on it. Just recently she has found out through the adoption agency that she also has a brother who is two years older. He was also given up for adoption. For me and Vonda it is just another similar thing in our lives that we share.

CHAPTER 19

God's House

Without any doubt, church has been the greatest positive force of influence in my life.

The love and spiritual education I have received has helped me to be a better husband, father, son, brother, friend and neighbor and has opened up the cocoon I was in and ushered me into a better world. The world was the same but my response to it was different. I was no longer the caterpillar slithering around limited in my ability to experience and understand because of my low vantage point. I was now a beautiful butterfly that scaled the trees and mountains and soared to heights that gave me the ability to see my present surroundings with greater context and peer in the distance at what awaits those who put their trust in Jesus at the end of the rainbow. When a person sees this truth, like I have, one can never be the same nor will they want to.

I had been a Christian in the neighborhood of five years before I started to attend the traditional Sunday morning church service. I wanted to go but I had a tri-fold problem that held me back. I was afraid of the holy unknown, I did not think I needed to go, and I simply refused to obey God's will in this area. Being afraid was a jellyfish (no backbone) lack of trust in God. Thinking I did not need to go was a lame self-delusional lie I accepted so I could run my own show and be the master of my life. And lastly stupidity, I rebelled against God and told him no. 'I know what is best for me more than you do' says the pottery to the potter. Besides, no one would care if I showed up.

Another thing that kept me from going was I never felt any emotional connection to a group and the benefits of going to church would surely not apply to me I thought. When I eventually grew a spine, stopped the self-deception and removed the stupid pride, I experienced that church should be the most desired place on earth that a person would want to be. If you claim to love God, then you/I have an opportunity on a weekly basis to hear God's words of encouragement, hope and instructions on what and how to live a life that is pleasing to him and be beneficial to mankind. Going to church is an opportunity to celebrate weekly what Jesus did for us and what he promises to do for us in the future, with other appreciative believers, with no respect to economic or social position and race. Church is a place where walls and moats that are built at work and in the community to protect us from others are carefully removed so we are free to be ourselves and begin the cleaning and shaping of our hidden diamond.

Lastly but not least, church cultivates and fosters a climate of deeper, richer and more rewarding personal relationships because there is no need to be anyone other than you. Church encourages everyone to leave their Superman cape at home and just come as Clark Kent. Why, because there is only one superhero and his name is Jesus. The beauty of a good bible believing and living church is that everyone, including Wade Oliver, Mr. Gray himself, fits in. Why, because everyone is a sinner, and on equal footing with God. The person who is sitting next to you, in front of you and even preaching from the pulpit has problems and pains just like I/you have. You are accepted as an equal in spite of that, and are free to be yourself. The liberating power of love that flows in and through church is what the devil does not want people to know.

My first experience of church was in California when Martin Zavala and his family invited me and brought me to their church. I wish I could say that I learned something like a bible verse or a golden nugget of wisdom, but the only thing I can remember is playing foosball and gazing down one day over the bathroom partition and seeing Martin flush the worlds longest unbroken #2 deposit. The fact that Martin did not hit me and that the toilet did not overflow would probably qualify as my first two church miracles. That was in fourth grade and I went a handful of times. When we moved back to Minnesota I went to a church service one other time and that was in the sixth grade.

A couple of adults had come to our apartment development and gave an invitation to me and all of the other kids to visit their church. They promised it would be lots of fun and that we would be given some candy. If you are fishing for fish you use worms. If you are fishing for kids you use the words fun and candy. I went and somewhere between the fifth and sixth minute of sitting in the pews listening to the pastor, I concluded that their idea of fun and my idea of fun did not match. I received my candy at the end of the night and that would be the last time they ever saw me again. Give me a spanking but please do not send me to church. The next time I would go to church would be involuntarily seven years later in the first week of my basic training in the US Air Force.

My hope is that everyone in life will have a Jeff Droll standing at one of their forks in the road of life with a road map and a bottle of cool refreshing lemonade waiting for them. Jeff would be the foam mallet that God used to hit me up side my head twelve years later to get me to go to church. Jeff and I worked the same graveyard shift on the same floor at the main post office and we became pretty good friends, or more accurately good Christian brothers. For about nine years we would meet together for lunch and breaks and talk about our shared faith. We spent many hours talking about scripture as well as praying for each other, our co-workers and our families. Early on in our relationship Jeff gave me an invitation to come and visit his church. From there it became a periodic shot of encouragement as well as a loving reminder that God wanted me to find a church to attend and dig roots. He wasn't telling me something that I didn't already know and want, but it just wasn't happening.

Fast forward about two years and Jeff gives me an invitation to bring Arias and Ajaa to his church Oak Hill Baptist Wednesday night children's ministry called AWANA. I would describe it as a boy scouts and girl scouts club that emphasizes bible memorization and bible teachings filled with lots of games. I took him up on his invitation to bring Arias and Ajaa. While everyone was in their respective groups and classes, I would walk around and watch what was going on. All of the kids and adults were having a blast. Before you know it I began to volunteer and my image of church changed from something questionable to something safe and fun. It was beautiful to be around other people who loved God and who wanted to serve others.

The next year I signed up to help assist with the Cubbies and then the following year I would be the Co-leader of Cubbies with my wife Vonda. Cubbies are a pre kindergarten age group of older three's and younger five year olds. Even though I would eventually start going to another church, I would continue bringing Arias, Ajaa and then Rico to Oak Hill for AWANA on Wednesday nights for the next four years, including some of our neighbor kids that lived on our block. There is much beauty and pleasure in witnessing the unhindered and unmasked actions of little kids.

They say what they think and do what they feel without concern for self or others. They live entirely in the moment. Only during these episodes in life can we truly say 'ignorance is bliss'. Substitute an adult in place of any of these little cubbies and childlike innocence is replaced with criminal behavior and/ or deep intellect and emotional problems.

When you are teaching and leading little three, four, and five year olds be prepared to laugh, exercise patience, and laugh some more. Here a few of the more memorable moments I have had with Cubbies through the AWANA programs I have been apart of. "Everyone it is time for story time. Please put the toys away and let's get into a circle. Elizabeth that is a very pretty dress you have on, but you are not supposed to wear it over your head. Please sit up like everyone else and put your dress down." Elizabeth would then flash her million-dollar smile, sit up and then pull her dress down. This would be repeated every couple of weeks. Vonda would tell her that ladies do not pull their dresses over their heads and that Elizabeth was a little lady. It always reminded me of Gary Larson's FARSIDE comic of what a person says and what a dog hears. "Fetch the stick Rover; fetch the stick Rover, good boy". The dog hears "blah, blah, blah Rover, blah, blah, blah, Rover, good boy!" Take out the Rover and put in Elizabeth and the actions and results were always the same. Our next little Cubby story stars Josh.

Everyone has their own coping mechanisms to deal with stressful and fearful situations. One of our cubbies had his own coping tool for shyness that Vonda and I thought was quite funny. Each night we would begin class by calling out the name of the cubby and they would be given an attendance star to put up by their name. Not every time, but quite often, Josh would be under the table hiding. After being coaxed to come out and place his star on the board he would then take his seat at the table like the rest of his cubby companions. I never told him this but for anyone who is shy and wants to become inconspicuous, hiding underneath a table is counter productive. Josh has since grown up and no longer hides underneath tables.

Awana is very organized with all lessons and activities for that week connected by a theme. Even in gym time there were recommended games to reinforce a bible story that was taught. One of the games was the simple 'Red light' 'Green light'. The kids start at one end of the gym and run towards me at the other end. When I say 'green light', they can run, when I say 'red light' they have to stop. If I turn around and see them running after saying 'red light', they have to go back to the beginning. I was either a poor explainer of the rules or it was a prophetic revelation about the future driving capacity of some of the cubbies, but there was a lot of red light driving.

Gym time is supposed to be fun and give the kids an opportunity to release some of their pent up energy. We had twenty minutes each night so learning any new game cut into their play time. Vonda would have a game picked out from a list of game choices for that week that related to our bible story. Between quieting the kids, helping them focus and repeating the game object and rules, we would only have about ten minutes left to play with them now having more anxiousness. I told Vonda that I had an idea that made it easier for her as well as the little cubbies. We would no longer restrict ourselves to the regimented game format but would simple bring a couple of balls inside the gym. The object of this game was very simple, you just run around screaming and laughing. You can run in circles, flap your arms, kick the ball, catch the ball or throw the ball. The kids loved it and for twenty minutes each gym period that is what we did. We had a few parents ask us what we did because their child was ready to hit the bed when they got home.

This last story is without a doubt my favorite one of all. The season was Christmas and the month was December. Vonda had called all of the little cubbies into a circle because we were going to sing some Christmas songs. Vonda selected a song and the whole group sang along. After we sang the song, Vonda asked them to name some of their favorite Christmas songs that they would like for us to sing. I didn't think they would be able to name any of the more traditional songs like 'Silent Night' or "Little town of Bethlehem", but I was sure one of them would say "Rudolph the red nosed reindeer", "Jingle bells", or "Frosty the snowman". What would be offered up as his favorite Christmas song would send me and Vonda to the floor gasping for air. His name was Elliot and he had always had that sheepish look that said " I didn't do it"; all the while you were looking at the canary feather protruding from his mouth. Elliot raised his hand and Vonda asked what his favorite Christmas song was so that we could sing it. Elliot put his hand down and then smiled. Without missing a note and on beat he sang the title of a current popular rap song being played on the radio. "Who let the dogs out? Woof, woof, woof, who let the dogs out? Woof, woof, woof." After thanking Elliot for his suggestion we told him that "Who let the dogs out" is not a Christmas song but he was welcome to suggest another.

Less than a year later after my positive experience and exposure to

Awana at Jeff's church, I began to attend 4th Baptist Church in North Minneapolis on Father's Day 1995. 4th Baptist was a large church that had a connected seminary as well as a small fm radio station. It was founded many years ago when all of the surrounding area was of European descent. Since that time, the area has changed into a varied ethnic melting pot with African American being the largest percentage of any ethnic group. A year later, 4th Baptist would later sell their church property including their radio frequency and buy some land and build a new church and seminary in Plymouth.

My first memory of Wade wanting and going to church as an adult would be here at 4th Baptist. After arriving late, I entered the sanctuary (worship area) and gazed around as to where I should sit. Everywhere looked full so I decided to walk to the second row up in the front and grab a seat. Only later in time after I would marry Vonda would I see the humor in what just happened. Within the four to five hundred people in attendance, only a handful of those people, and I being a part of that handful, were people that had melanin in our skin.

Next, I was clueless about the basic church dress decorum one should try to wear if one has any of those clothes in their possession; which so happened I did not. Most everyone in church was wearing a dress and if they were not wearing a suit at the minimum they had on a pair of slacks with a shirt and tie. I strolled in oblivious to what anyone was wearing and sat down in my sleeveless muscle shirt and camouflaged sleeveless winter jacket. I received a few hellos and smiles and felt like I had been there forever. The music was great, the preaching was great and my first day of church was beautiful. God had thought of everything in regards to my seat assignment. What better encouragement on someone's first day at church than placing them in front of the state's #1 tone deaf, scratchy throat, eardrum breaking singer so as to make me, the #2 in the state feel o.k. I began to faithfully attend without Apple throughout the remainder of the year. Apple and I were having marital problems so it was just my bible and I. In January of 1996 a month after my divorce, Vonda and I began to go church together.

On our first visit we walked up to the second row and sat down. Vonda took off her coat to reveal her beautiful dress, and I took off my zippered sweat jacket with camouflage vest jacket and showed off my beautiful sleeveless muscle shirt. Vonda said she almost had a heart attack. It would be the last time I would ever go to church that dressed down again. Vonda made sure of it. Thank you honey for breaking the figurative ammonia pill, and putting it under my nose; I must have been going to church in a semi conscious state. Throughout our marriage Vonda would use other devices such as sledgehammers, cherry-bombs, water boarding, bamboo shards underneath the fingernails and much patience to help me break through some of my other peculiarities. "Just because everyone else does it and I am the only person who doesn't, does not mean they are right." I would say.

In 1996, 4th Baptist Church moved and left behind a satellite church to continue to minister and serve the people there. Family Baptist would become the name of this new church and Vonda, our children and I would be part of this new team. It was an exciting time for me because of the many opportunities I was given to minister to people. My fondest memory of Family Baptist is what God did in the life of a man who from the world's perspective had it all. He was a very successful executive who traveled and pulled in a very healthy paycheck. Providing for his large family and living comfortable would never be an issue he would ever have to worry about. The beauty of the story is that he responded to the will of God to quit his job and go into the seminary to get trained to become the pastor of Family Baptist. It was not an instantaneous decision but in time he said yes to God and no to himself. He left the safety of the suburbs and moved his white family into the heart of the lions den of violence, drugs, gang activity and broken family units.

If this is not evidence of the reality of and transformational power of Jesus, there is nothing a non-believer will accept. Only through the power and love of God, could a person do that, and would want to do something like that. Jesus showed the nail holes in his hands to 'doubting' Thomas one of the twelve apostles because Thomas did not believe that Jesus actually was resurrected. Jesus said to Thomas after he had looked at and touched the nail holes, "because you have seen me you have believed; blessed are those (in the future) who have not seen and yet have believed."

We met many new people and made a lot of friends; but after a few years of faithful service and support we felt a nudge by God to move to another church. We bounced around for a few years trying to find the right church for us, and eventually God led us to Brooklyn Park Evangelical Free Church. Sr. Pastor Rick Ensrud and the rest of the ministry staff are wonderful people and have been a blessing in my life. To all of the wonderful pastoral staff and congregation at B.P.E.F.C, "thank you"; but the number one person who deserves thanks is my wonderful wife Vonda. She has been a dynamo in her efforts to make sure the kids were involved in church and was a great encouragement to me as I watched her volunteer to help in many ways. Because of her concern and effort our kids and I are better people. Lastly I want to thank the many unnamed people I have met at church who befriended me and loved me and gave me an opportunity to experience the pleasure of learning and serving others.

CHAPTER 20

Aliens at the Post Office

I have wrestled periodically with discontentment while working for the post office throughout the years I have been there. If it was not related to the hours of the day I worked, the forced overtime I had to do, or the days off, then it was because of the same ole, same ole, of the job. Wanting something fresh that offered new challenges and personal growth opportunity led me from a distribution clerk to that of a Sales & Service associate to a delivery supervisor and finally my current position of an Address Mgmt specialist.

The majority of all mail distribution at post office processing plants occurs during the window of 9pm – 6am. Being hired as a distribution clerk meant I would have to disrupt and turn on my head the normal human schedule of sleeping and social life. This would eventually lead to my current insomnia. My first three years of singleness and being a non-Christian antagonized and fought against what should have been a good attitude and faithful attendance. After getting married to Apple and having Arias and Ajaa, I grew to appreciate the graveyard shift as a blessing. I understood that it gave me twice as much time if not more to be with my kids than the typical father who worked the Dolly Parton 9-5 day shift.

After my divorce form Apple and my re-marriage to Vonda the graveyard shift became not as family friendly. With the kids now going to school and growing up, there were becoming more and more evening social events that crossed into my 'downtime' before I went to work causing me and Vonda some anxieties. In addition Vonda found it a royal pain in the butt to walk on eggshells and keep the kids quiet when I was sleeping during the day. So after thirteen years of working the graveyard shift I began to look for a day job.

I applied for a Sales & Service assoc. position that had split days off. It was in the farthest Southern frontier of the Minneapolis delivery area in West Bloomington at the West Bloomington Branch. The name would later be officially changed to the Thomas Burnett Jr. Branch in honor of this man who lost his life in a valiant effort to wrestle control from the Islamic terrorists in one of the planes that crashed on the infamous day of September 11th; a.k.a. 911. After I passed the required training, I officially left the zombie night life of the postal service and entered into the sunshine existence of regular life. For the next four years I was content, happy and at peace until I had an inner prodding for a new challenge. It was time to move forward and I had set my eyes on becoming a delivery station supervisor with hopes of spring boarding into a delivery station manager or small postmaster position. It would take about fourteen months and three interview attempts before a review board, before I finally received the new challenge I was after.

I had scored very high on the written part of the test (not that it was to difficult) and demonstrated the ability to perform the requirements of the job by submitting written situations where I had done similar type requirements in past jobs and/or my current job, including non-profit organizations like church, and this gave me cause to be confident and optimistic heading into my first interview. The interview came and went and I waited for the verdict. A couple of weeks later I received a "Dear John" letter that said thank you for applying but you were not accepted. After a few days of being in the dumps I picked myself off of the ground, changed my attitude and told myself to go at it again. I made a phone call to one of the review panel members and asked her why I fell short and what could I do to improve my position for the next time. She said that I had no supervisory experience and that I would need to submit a better demonstrative example for one of the specific requirements.

I told my boss what she had said and I asked him if I could get a little supervising under my belt. He made a couple of phone calls and lined it up for me to go to another post office for a couple of weeks for some supervisor training. I have a boatload of respect and admiration for Mark Weingartz who has since retired as the Mgr of Thomas Burnett Jr. Branch. He had a small piece of paper posted by his door in his office that said, "People may forget what you said and they may forget what you did.

But, people will never forget how you made them feel". Mark made me feel wonderful and I will always treasure those feelings.

Months later I applied again and earned an opportunity to sit before the review panel that would give thumbs up or thumbs down for my advancement. Because I had a brief stint of 'Customer Service' supervision under my belt and had improved on a couple of my responses to the 'job requirements' portion of the job application, I went in with even more confidence and optimism than the preceding time. The interview ended with handshakes and smiles and I left feeling better than the first time. Every day after I came home from work, I checked the mail hoping that the letter would be in the mailbox. After a couple of weeks of waiting, the letter finally came. I slowly opened it up visualizing it saying congratulations. Instead, it was another "Dear John" letter. I had failed again and this time it hurt a lot more.

So after a few days of self pity, I peeled my ego off of the floor once again to go at it again. Perseverance builds character and God was helping me grow in maturity. It is never fun but that is the way it is. *"Faith is the evidence of things hoped for without the evidence of things seen"* and God spoke to my spirit and promised me that it was going to happen after I had finished reading Joshua Chapter 1 during a quiet devotional. Because of the inner spiritual assurance I had, I was more than optimistic about receiving a 'congratulations letter' next time.

I made the phone call for the second time, but this time I spoke to the head review committee member. I asked him why he had rejected me. He told me that he felt I was too nice of a guy who would be unwilling to handle the most difficult part of the job which is interpersonal persuasion and corrective discipline to the 3% of the workforce that causes 95% of the problems. (He did not say the 3% and 95% that is just my opinion). I told him of the differing coaching styles of two recent Superbowl winning coaches. My style leaned more towards Tony Dungy and less like Bill Cowher. I told him nobody enjoys that part of the job including me, but if the situation arose and called for a confrontation I would not shrink back or bury my head in the sand hoping the problem would go away. Months later I would apply again and be given another interview opportunity to try and persuade the review panel that the USPS would benefit if they promoted me to a Customer Service supervisor. Being persistent paid off and on my third attempt, the letter in the mailbox said "Congratulations". After four months of classroom and on the job training I became a Customer Service supervisor.

There is an old saying 'be careful of what you wish for'. In fashion with the old 1960 television detective series called 'Dragnet', the names and places of this real life event has been changed to protect the innocent.; namely me. His name was Dufus McGee and Dufus worked as a clerk at the Happyville Post office in Happyville. The glass was always half empty in Dufus' world, causing him to act like a bain in the putt. On this particular day I was sitting at my desk in the middle of the workroom floor when I had asked Dufus to do a necessary task. Dufus being a Dufus, just stood in my face and told me no. Dufus' glass was empty and when it was empty he disliked authority and anything else that breathed oxygen.

I asked Dufus again, but Dufus did a double dufus and said no with more attitude. Realizing I was dealing with a fifty-year-old 1st grader, I gave Dufus a direct order and told him if he did not comply I would call the police and have him escorted out of the building. That was my final raise. My guess is that Dufus had previously seen the 'World Series of Poker' on cable t.v. and thought he had the winning hand with his dual 'eights' and dual 'aces' so he threw everything in and called. I laid down my direct order and it showed three 'in your face' Bill Cowher's and two 'soft spoken' Tony Dungy's. My full house beat his two pair. The police came and Dufus was escorted out of the building giving the post office a temporary increase in production as the 3% fell to 2.99978%.

In the vicinity of the 3% is another category of challenge and that is the category of discomfort. An unhappy employee brought it to my attention that a specific employee was not flushing their business after relieving themselves in the bathroom. They asked me to have a talk with this person instructing them on the obvious. I spoke with the accused in my Tony Dungy disposition and told him what was told to me giving him a chance to deny or clarify. He told me that he did not flush because he believed in water conservation. I told him that the USPS has made provisions in their budget to pay for a single flush per bathroom visit. Also besides being gross, no one wants to come behind someone and make a deposit on their deposit. He agreed reluctantly to comply but a week later I had to use a Bill Cowher approach. I made it clear that I did not want to have this conversation again. I am no longer a delivery supervisor and I would be lying if I said I miss the pressures of the 3%, long hours and the almost daily duty of putting out the 'on the job' fires of delivery station challenges. God pulled some strings (all of my undeserved fortune is attributed to God's grace) and I was awarded a position as an Address

Management Specialist. I work with a group of outstanding people who are professional, team oriented, and have a wonderful sense of humor.

Setting the dials to the year 1987, we will take a ride in the postal time machine and travel back to the beginning of my postal career where I started as a LSM operator. The LSM stands for letter-sorting-machine. When you were awake and had music to listen to, the job was not so bad. Sitting at a keyboard console typing a two digit number on a letter that swept by you at a one second time interval eventually became mind numbing. It also created a pinched nerve in my neck that forced me to go to the manual unit about two years later where I would work until getting my day job. It did not take long for me to disturb the symbiotic flow of life on the LSM with the people in my zone I worked with. Initially the incident was not funny but time usually changes the perspective of things. It reminds me of my first impression I had given to my new colleagues at my first duty base in the Air Force.

The LSM machine had about fifteen consoles for keying and about three different zip codes on at any one time. The function of the LSM machine sorted letter mail to each individual carrier at a higher rate of production compared to manual sortation. We had a rotation of five people on four consoles. Every thirty minutes we would be relieved to go to the back of the machine for ten minutes to empty the full bins of letters and put them in the labeled carrier trays. On my second day I noticed that Julio (fictitious name) always sat on console number four and had his own rotation. He got up anytime he wanted and went down to the end of the machine and had a cigarette.

Albert Einstein I am not, but it did not take a nuclear physicist to figure out that seat number four was the better of the four seats to sit in. I said to myself that is the seat I will sit in from now on. The next day I got there a little early and plopped into seat number four. After keying for awhile I got out of my seat and went down to the end of the machine like Julio did; knowing all the while cold vicious imaginary knives were being hurled at me from behind. When I came back World War 3 took place. I told the group I don't care if you have had that rotation for all of the years you say you have, I am here now and we will do it the fair way. Julio did not like it and eventually bid off and went somewhere else. From that day forward we made amends to the rotation and chair number four was part of it.

In the manual unit on the third floor I was assigned to zip code 55431 and later 55432. Initially the manual unit had a very large number of workers but has since been shrunk to almost nil due to the technological advance of automation. I had many fond memories working in this area whereas it gave me great opportunity to talk with many people who worked side by side with me. I had many discussions about God, sports, and other stuff and laughed quite often. Sometimes the laughing was not as a result of something that was said, but the head scratching behavior of some of the people that worked there. A few years ago there was a movie starring Will Smith called 'Men in Black'. In the movie there is a scene where an alien is disguised as a post office backroom clerk. For once Hollywood finally got it right. This part of the movie is actually an accurate depiction of your average night worker at a postal plant. If I had a nickel for every time I laughed at my alien co-workers, I would be a very wealthy man. Truth be told, some of those aliens also thought I was from another world too.

After thirteen years of clerking I moved on to become a Sales & Service Associate. This is the title of a job in the clerk craft that works behind the counter at post offices. Besides the difference in the hours of the day I worked, the most notable change between the manual clerk position I had and the Sales & Service Associate position was that of contact with the public. It was refreshing and enjoyable to meet and converse with the thousands of customers I had over my five year period, many of which were wonderfully kind, friendly and funny. To my surprise I discovered that the post office does not have a monopoly on extraterrestrials. Some of the aliens from other planets who did not work for the USPS would come to the post office to buy stamps and mail packages to other planets in our solar system. Here are a couple special moments in my twenty-two year postal career.

This first one is very special to me. This proud moment happened only because God made a change in my heart and mind that gave me the strength and desire to do the right thing. The old gray Wade would have never done this. Somewhere in the 1990's a person had drawn a picture of a person hanging in a noose in the stairwell at the Main Post Office in Minneapolis where I was working. The nationality of the person in the noose was interpreted to be a person of African ancestry. I never saw it but a few of the people of African American descent who did took great offense. When will we get rid of the divisive designators that we use to describe non-Caucasian people? Will our supposed higher intelligent social scientists ever figure it out that as long as we continue to label and group people we will never become united and color blind? Martin Luther

King Jr. had a dream that one day men and women would be judged by the character of their lives and not by the color of our skin. It makes me want to vomit. I am a man, then a Christian, and then an 'American'.

The custodial staff cleaned the wall and removed the offensive drawing within a few days. How many people saw it, I do not know, but most people in the building rode the elevator up and down versus walking the stairwell anyway, so my guess is not that many people of all the working ethnic groups had actually seen it. Everyone has a right to feel what they want, and as for me I took no offense at all. Someone who would draw something that is derogatory towards a person or group of people only demonstrates that they are the one with the problem not the intended target. I won't go into any details, but it snowballed into a class action lawsuit against the USPS. It was not their fault but you know lawyers.

About two years later I received a letter from a lawyer who was filing the class action suit. It was sent out to every person of African lineage who was working at the main post office at the time. The letter requested my input to any emotional pain I may have received because of this incident. It said if I do not respond I would be ineligible for any cash settlement in the future. I tore up the letter and threw it in the garbage. A year or so later I received another letter that said I have another opportunity to sign on to be apart of the class action lawsuit. Like the first letter, I tore it into pieces and threw it into the garbage. All it did was make me angry. I thought about the lady who purchased a hot cup of coffee from McDonalds (exactly what she wanted), and when she had put the cup between her legs and accidentally spilled it and burned herself, she successfully sued McDonalds and was awarded a very large sum of money. How was it McDonalds fault, or in this case how is the USPS responsible for some idiot who scribbled on the wall? I shook my head and said I will have no part with those white collar legalized criminals called lawyers.

When I had totally forgotten about it, a few years later I received my last letter. It said that the class action lawsuit had been won and that I am entitled to a share of the punitive damages. My share would be around $2000.00. All I would have to do is sign the papers, send them back and I would receive the money. Everything would be confidential so no one in management or the union will ever know. My family has always lived paycheck to paycheck, so the extra money would have been like a lottery win. For about a half hour I was pacing back in forth in my living room trying to convince myself that it would be o.k. for me to sign. Instead of signing the letter, just like the first two letters, I tore it up into pieces and threw it in the garbage. Because I knew in my heart I did the right thing, I was rewarded with a good conscience and filled with a little pride. Besides the lawsuit being bogus from the beginning in my opinion, God showed me that I would actually be robbing from the company that feeds my family. All credit goes to God.

This next one is a witness to the goodness of some of the wonderful customers I have had and their sense of humor they possess. It will also reveal my disease of 'Foot in Mouth' that flares up every once in awhile. Remember, when life throws you lemons, make lemonade. On this occasion a customer did just that. I had inadvertently tossed a lemon his way and he cut it up, added some sugar and served a great tasting drink. It was another beautiful day in the neighborhood that had me manning my post at window #1 with my late colleague and friend Ruth Jones in window #2. A gentleman came to the Post office to mail a small item and was perusing through our packaging supplies when he looked at me and asked for my recommendation on the best package. I said "sir if you choose that package hanging over there versus the one you are holding, it will save you an arm and a leg."

Now all of you generation X people like me who grew up watching the Flintstones should remember this one with Fred. Fred was in Mr. Slate's office (his boss) getting congratulated for an act of benevolence he did. While Mr. Slate was talking, Fred began to shrink down to the size of a mouse because he had undone his action and realized he had made a giant mistake that would eventually turn his bosses praise into contempt. As soon as I said that I began to shrink. Now why I said that will be soon revealed, the fact is in the three years at the window I had never used that phrase with any of my customers.

Now while I was shrinking and before he would respond, I was hoping that he and everyone else in ear shot did not really make the connection of my goof. That soon disappeared as Ruth who was trying to be inconspicuous was telling me "Wade he only has one leg." I pretended not to hear her so that the situation would disappear and end, but she interpreted my non-acknowledgement as a sign that she needed to say it again but only louder. I told her under my breath that I know. But she did not hear me so she said it again, louder than the last time. What she didn't know is that because she is hard of hearing her comments were loud enough for me and everyone else in the vicinity to hear the first time as well as the second and third. Finally, the gentleman looked at me and calmly said, "I can afford to lose an arm but not another leg." I told him it was a slip of the tongue and apologized. He graciously accepted my apology with a smile.

Incident #3 is one of my favorites and falls in the 'America's funniest video' range. Working a couple of windows down from me was a very charismatic and smart man named Dave. Dave became a part time 'Sales & Service Associate a couple of years after I did and stayed about six months until he decided to go back to the plant. Dave did all of the duties a Sales & Service Associate did. He educated the customers on their mailing options and types of delivery service we offered, as well as assisting them with any other mailing questions and needs. The only difference between Dave and I was he was deaf. He had completely lost his hearing about eight years prior through some disease. Dave had learned how to read lips and he was very good at it. When customers would approach his window, he would let them know that he was deaf and that he read lips if they were not facing him. It was a slow day and at this time I had no customer to wait on so I just stood in my area waiting, watching and listening.

An older gentleman came to Dave's window to mail an already filled out Express mail envelope. Because he did not need the recipient to sign for it, Dave told him that he could sign the waiver to exempt the signature and pointed to that area. The older man grabbed the envelope and slid it closer to himself on the counter. Dave stood and waited for him to sign it. As the old man was gazing downward he told Dave that he was blind and could not see it. Dave did not hear him so Dave did not respond. The older man said he was blind again and Dave said that he needed to look at him because he was deaf. The older guy didn't hear him clearly and said "what". This went on for a couple more exchanges until they both were on the same page. For me this was one of the funniest things I have ever witnessed. I was not laughing because of their physical challenges but that it was something in the neighborhood of an old comedy movie I had seen starring Richard Pryor and Gene Wilder. Richard was blind and Gene was deaf and some of the communication mishaps that happened in the movie were similar to what I just witnessed.

I started with my proudest moment and will end with my least favorite. I was working with a guy who for reasons known only to him felt it necessary to do clandestine harassment actions towards me as well as display open disrespect. I have my reasons as to why he was doing them, (all unfavorably towards him) but I will keep silent. This harassment and non-professional work relationship went on for about a year and a half. What made this difficult was he was the lead 'Sales & Service Assoc. and

I had to deal with him infrequently in the course of my daily duties. Most of his maliciousness, unprofessionalism and disrespect that he did towards me I kept silent on. A handful of times I told my boss but nothing ever changed.

In the course of every year, the USPS has mandated safety talks, training, and reminders of postal rules and regulations that all employees read and/or listen to. On this occasion there was a video presentation on workplace violence. The video affirmed the USPS position that no workplace violence was tolerated. This included threats of violence as well as any physical altercations. The USPS has established a 'zero tolerance' and any such grievances would be subject to removal and permanent dismissal. I watched it and I was in full agreement. After viewing I signed the sheet of paper that now made me accountable. What makes this laughable is that in less than 24 hours I would violate this.

The next day Mr. 'not so nice guy' purposely bumped into me while we were walking opposite ways through an aisle. I took offense to it and told him "the next time you do anything else to me, I am going to kill you." It was the straw that broke the camel's back. I really wanted to pummel him, but I couldn't because of the zero tolerance. As soon as I said that, I said inside my head "uh ooh, I have just blown it." I knew I had to immediately tell my boss before the 'not so nice person' did, so I walked back into the boss's office and told him what had just happened. After I was in there for about forty seconds, the 'not so nice guy' saw me talking with the boss and realized he had a golden opportunity to get me in some deep trouble. He knew why I said what I said and that it was only an emotional slip of the tongue, but that was not how he played.

So he walked into the office and told the boss I had threatened to kill him. My boss had no option but to punch us both off the clock and send the both of us home. I was at home without pay for three weeks. The 'not so nice guy' went back to work a few days later. While I was at home, I had deep anxieties because I was under the impression that they were going to fire me because of the 'zero tolerance' with them not realizing there were extenuating circumstances that made this an exception. During my hiatus at home an investigation was done and I was eventually vindicated. Thankfully some of my co-workers had told the investigator/s some of the harassment they had witnessed which supported what I had been telling my boss all along. I came back to work and a couple of months later the 'not so nice guy' left to work at another station.

Before it was settled and while I was at home waiting for what the post office was going to do, my mother and her friend Gwen both who are not in the best physical shape were going to recruit a bunch of people who live in their senior high-rise and picket in front of the post office demanding justice. It would have been quite a seen seeing about fifteen or more gray hairs holding signs and driving their little scooters. I am glad they did not have to do that, but it is really cool to know that they were willing to do that for me.

To all of the hundreds of people in the USPS who have given me a smile and have shown me kindness, thank you!!! In addition to my employment at the USPS, I have recently begun to work part-time as an advocate in a four unit apartment building for men and women with mental disabilities. This is a new chapter in my life that I am excited about. On one of the days I was working I was driving back to the apartment with one of the men. In conversation I had asked him if he knew where he was going after he died. Without pondering and in a matter of fact way said, "Yeah, I think the cemetery". In many ways they are so much more in tune with living then us so called 'normal' people. Maybe one day I will be able to write about the struggles they overcome and their high level appreciation of the simple things in life that most of us take for granted.

CHAPTER 21

Full Circle

I tried with much effort to make Jesus the focal point of our lives individually and collectively as a family. We had family bible studies, prayed together and got involved in church activities and ministries. There was no such thing as a 'separation between church and state'. God was not compartmentalized and brought out on special occasions like fine china at a holiday dinner. The bible teaches that God is a 24/7 God, concerned about every minute in our day. Just as eating, drinking, resting and breathing are essential in the 24 hour time cycle, so too is the necessity for daily interchange with the Spirit of God and our spirit. God's word teaches that God is deserving of continual praise, is concerned with every problem we have no matter how small, and that we should pray for wisdom, guidance, protection, courage and forgiveness throughout the day as needed. It is scary to think how my life and family would have turned out without Jesus in it. Jesus is not a placebo mental pill like some people imagine. I know first hand what it is like to not have him in my life and every other believer will tell you the same thing.

In addition to the spiritual component of our family's priorities, another thing that was emphasized was making sure the kids received quality education. Because of the hawkish monitoring of Vonda, her communication with our kid's teachers and her involvement in the school functions and activities are kids did very well. Rico and Ajaa were straight 'A' students in High School with the occasional 'B'; while Arias received the occasional 'A' accompanied with 'B's and 'C's. Two of them did it because they wanted to, and the other one did it because he had to. Moms and dads out there stay on top of your kid's education. Raise the bar high and they will do it.

The third leg of the chair that our family rested on was sports. Right from the beginning all of our kids began to play in organized sports including basketball, baseball, softball, tennis, track, soccer, volleyball and football through High School. They were all very good athletes and it was very enjoyable watching them play. Vonda was their number one cheerleader with me a close second. It began early with the plastic bat and ball and the indoor adjustable four foot high basketball hoop. Arias was a natural at two years of age. I remember seeing an old 'Saturday Night Live' sketch poking fun at Earl Woods; Tiger Woods dad. As Tiger began to excel and win, a cash register sound of cha-ching would go off in Earl's head suggesting his son was his pot of gold at the end of the rainbow. I did not think about the pot of gold but I did sit in awe and marvel at his talent in basketball, baseball and football. I was positive he would go professional in something but practicing was not at the top of his list. Early on Arias was a one man wrecking crew at point guard on his basketball teams. For someone who did not like baseball he was almost un-hittable as a pitcher and a vacuum at shortstop. He is one of the most gifted young athletes I have ever seen.

Ajaa came out of the blocks a little slower than Arias, but after her intro to gymnastics at four, ball skills at five, a few years of basketball, and her two year dance stint at Kay Marie & Carol's Dance Studio (all for the express purpose of getting a trophy), she would find her niche in volleyball and softball. Her favorite sport was softball where she shined as bright as the sun. Her first organized sports began in Little League where she was one of only a handful of girls. In the B-minor level she completed dominated as she was one of the strongest players in the league. She launched many bombs including one out to the parking lot that had her rounding 3rd base before the outfielder even touched the ball. Sadly as she moved up she was unjustly passed over in the all-star selection unlike her two brothers. We had won a few championships and she was arguable the best hitter on the team. In our first championship in the A-minor league she was 7 for 7 with three triples, three doubles and a single in the last two games including the championship game. She rocked!!!!

Rico was and still is a very good athlete who excelled in baseball and football up to the 8th grade. Rico was always the fastest or one of the fastest players on the field but his lack of size would become a challenge. Rico gave up playing football in 8th grade after running into the opposing 300 lb lineman on the other team. When you are only 130 lbs dripping wet, fear and the law of gravity become a reality when you are squashed by people twice the size of you. Five years later he tried out for his college's football team at the running back position, but became disenchanted and quit because the practices became to boring. Because I was coaching Ajaa and Arias I saw very few of Rico's baseball games. The fact that he made the all-star team every year in Little League says enough. When I did watch Rico, he had the best eye, always made contact, and like Joe Mauer almost never struck out. When the three of them went to a small private Christian school for their middle school years, Rico would be one of the main cogs in the engine as Woodcrest beat up the other schools in basketball and soccer.

I coached three years of Arias & Rico's football team, four years of Little League baseball with Ajaa, with years two and three including Arias. I also coached one year each of basketball for both Arias and Rico. I had a lot of fun and met many nice people. Football and baseball started with a bang and ended with a dud. My first year as coach in football led to a perfect season with Arias, Rico and team steamrolling through the season and winning the championship. If there were any problems they were overlooked because winning does that. In our last year it was the complete opposite. We finished the season without a win and in most of the games we were unable to cross the fifty-yard line with our offense. We were overmatched in size, speed, strength and ability. In an attempt to motivate them I called them sissy's hoping that would make them mad and stoke their flames to burn hotter. Instead it made a few parents mad who were in the outer ring of the huddle. I apologized later when one of them told me I was wrong for saying what I said. It was one of my low points.

A parallel moment would happen in baseball. In the second and third year of coaching with Arias and Ajaa on the team we had finished in 1st place winning the championship. Life was great with very few problems. In my last year I had such an unpleasant coaching experience that I told myself I would never coach again and I haven't since. It started out with me asking one of the parents of the kids whom I did not like, and who was passed over by me to be the head coach, to coach with me as an assistant coach. We had a little history when the football team I coached with Arias and Rico pummeled the football team he coached with his son on it. It was an olive branch of peace gesture but was also my attempt to see if the saying, 'keep your friends close, but your enemy's closer' was true.

It only lasted a few games before we butted heads and I told him he needed to leave as coach. He was one of those fathers who got kicked out of the ballpark on more than one occasion by the umpire for his refusal to stop being disrespectful towards him about his umpiring performance. In the middle of the season I had one of my players fathers tell me that I was not attempting as many stolen bases as I did in years past. I told him this was a higher level of competition that prevented me from being as aggressive. He did not like my response and our relationship was soured the rest of the year. ¾ into the season I had another disgruntled father rock the boat. What hurt the most was he was someone I thought a friend who had my back, a Christian, and one of my assistant coaches. Someone had told me he was venting out by the bleachers during the game complaining about some coaching decision I had just made. Losing was creating a cancer and it was spreading close to the heart. I was o.k. with losing as long as the kids were trying, having fun and being positive.

Besides battling a few of the dads I also had a few malcontents that I had to continually discipline including one who I had to suspend to get his attention. This is Little League baseball, what is going on? The season began with high expectations from many of the parents. After a few practices I recognized we were a team that had mid-level talent at best. I thought it would be a smart thing to send out a letter before our first game saying I was completely committed to teaching their kids good sportsmanship, baseball skills while striving to win, but there was a likelihood that we might not win to many games and I needed there help to ensure they and their kids had fun. A few days later I was excoriated by a few of the parents. My prophetic warning was not embraced and the season went from a headache to a migraine.

Our kids sports have come to an end and no longer will Vonda and I be able to stand on the sidelines or sit in the bleachers cheering and watching our children play in competitive organized team youth games. The baby of the family, Ajaa, graduated from high school and the last page in that chapter has been turned and read.

As a family we were able to take a few mini vacations up north and once had taken a week long trip to Wisconsin at a family bible camp. I wanted to do so much more like take them to Disneyland or travel to some other states but we never had a lot of extra money. Life was still good and full in spite of the limited traveling we did. In regards to not having extra money, it was not due to wasteful spending but Vonda and my commitment to faithfully tithe to our church as well as pay for private education for our kids when they were in 6th -10th grade. If taxes were not so dang high, we would have had more money to spend and infuse into the economy. Hmmm, I have an idea, lower taxes so families and individuals have more money to buy products, services, and give to charities.

Time has flown by and the kids are no longer kids, but are now young adults. Rico has finished his third year of college at Northwestern College majoring in kinesiology. On June 16th, 2009 he began his first day of Air Force Reserves and flew down to Lackland AFB in San Antonio, Texas. Arias graduated high school in 2008 and enlisted in the US Marines. On July 27, 2009 he left for basic training at Camp Pendleton in San Diego, California. He will go full time active duty and after all of his training will more than likely be deployed to Afghanistan. The baby of the family Ajaa, graduated from Spring Lake Park High School in 2009 and has completed her first year of college at the University of Minnesota. In the past year she has gone from choosing her line of study from C.S.I. forensics, to Radiology to dentistry and back to sport science. It will be fun to see what her career will be.

Like all families we have had obstacles along the way; but when I look back, I see that because we had invited Jesus into our lives as our pilot, He had installed super high performance shocks and struts on our traveling vessel smoothing out our ride along the bumpy roads of life. My kids were given a better life than I had, and isn't that the dream of every parent? I love my kids very much because of who they are and because they gave me the greatest gift of all, an opportunity to be a dad.

Vonda has been my loving wife, friend, and "honey do list maker". She has been by my side supporting me and helping me grow in so many ways. Arias, Ajaa and Rico's lives have been blessed because of her love, sweat and tears. She has been a wonderful mother to Arias and Ajaa her two non-biological children. She has treated them as her own flesh and blood kids. All three have a golden future because of her and this is a major part of why I love her. Vonda has just completed her second marathon 12k (go on girl), and has found her way back into the healthcare community. In this struggling economy with many people out of work, God blessed her and she is now back at work as a LPN at Park Nicollet Hospital. This is whom she worked for when we met, but gave it up to have more time to raise our kids.

Claire my step dad died exactly one day after Apple died in June 1998. I think about him periodically and daydream about what could have been.

Sept 9, 2008, Harvey died and I felt no sadness. I had no idea that he was dying of cancer and I guess he wanted it that way. I called Cory and Mom and told them I was indecisive about making a presence at his funeral. After musing on it for a day, I came to the decision that my going was all about paying my respect to my sisters. Cory had initially said no to going, but after I told him I was going and the reasons I was going he changed his position as well. Cory called me a few hours later and said that he had stopped over Harvey's house and had a sit down chat with his/our three half-sisters whom we never see. (Of my three half sisters I had the joy of getting to spend a little time with my oldest sister Diane after Vonda and I got married. I enjoyed every minute I had with her). Cory told me something that was very surprising but not really. In the course of their group conversation they had shared with each other that they all were not as grief filled as one would expect at the passing of their father. One or all of them had said that Harvey was not the greatest father in the world.

I have only been to a handful of funerals but this one was quite unusual. Of the seven or eight people that stood up to say something about Harvey, all but one had prefaced their comments with "he was a difficult person". I went to the funeral to pay my last respects and I had no other motive than that. Harvey had made sure that if Cory or I had any other motive like inheriting any of his possessions, we had better think again. He had legally put it in his will to block Cory and me from all of his assets. I found this out through Cory who had received a call from an attorney after the funeral who represented the other heirs (our sisters). To me it really was not a surprise. I have no hate for Harvey only sympathy. In his attempt to deprive me of any of his estate, he overlooked the fact that I have everything that is of value and something he never had. I have a loving wife, beautiful God fearing kids who love me and I have a relationship with the living God who owns everything that exists. Harvey meant to hurt me but he only hurt himself. He went to his grave with hate and it will torment him forever. That is sad. A few weeks after going to Harvey's funeral I received a thank you card for my attendance at my own father's funeral. Forrest Gump was right "life is like a box of chocolates, you never know what you'll get".

Mom lives in the same city of Robbinsdale that I live in. Her health is poor, but she is still ticking. Besides the life time of love she has given me she has also provided me with much of my early life recall. Mom has long ago realized that her selection of men has not been good, so she has wisely chosen to only keep the company of Lucy her cat.

Everyone has a first memory and the general age of that first memory is between two and four years of age. Is this first memory a result of a neural connection in the brain that has finally grown and triggered the start of our memory bank? Is the first memory an ultra special moment that has happened in the middle of commonplace? Does anybody really know? I don't think so. Why is my first memory that of the art easel and the few wrapped presents? Were these the first presents I had ever received and this is why I remember? Had I been pleading to my mother to buy me an art easel so I can hone my savant like painting skill? The answers to both are no. I have concluded that the memories of life start there for me for this reason. The easel was symbolic of the 'Wizard of Oz' (black, white, gray and then Technicolor) life I would paint. Some of the paintings would be Picasso like that did not make any sense. These paintings showed my out of bounds behavior and attitude. Other paintings would be in the art form of realism showing how God was always there with me, walking side by side or carrying me when I was too tired or to hurt to walk in my own strength. These two groups of paintings were primarily painted in gray. When I became a Christian the gray gave way to an explosion of color.

The last group of paintings was painted in a fantasy dreamlike style. The colors that were used were colors I have never seen before and are brighter than the sun. These fantasy paintings showed the magical dreamlike world of heaven with all its perfection, with God at its center. In these paintings there was no more death, mourning, crying or pain; only unparalleled ceaseless joy. The few presents that were wrapped and sitting next to the easel were symbols of the many gifts I would receive in life; God, my family, my health, my friends, my job and discovering who I am and why I exist.

What color is peacefulness, soundness of mind, joy, love and hope? Whatever color it is, it now is the color of my soul. ***<u>I was born gray, but gray I am no more!</u>***

Call me blessed! Ajaa, Rico, Arias, Vonda and me.

CONCLUSION

Who I am and who you are starts at the beginning of the bible in the book of Genesis. On the last day of God's creative work week he created Adam the first man. Soon after, God would create Eve the first woman. They were innocent, pure and had a personal intimate relationship with the God of the universe. They were given the most laid back and least stressful job one could ever have. God placed them in the middle of the Garden of Eden and tasked them with the caretaking of the most beautiful garden in the history of the world. We can only imagine how jaw dropping beautiful it must have been. They were given freedom to do anything they wanted except one thing; that was to not eat from the tree of the knowledge of good and evil. This tree was nothing more than a trust tester, obedience measurer and a device that gave them free will and the opportunity to say no to God. God warned Adam and Eve and said that if they chose to eat from it there will be dire consequences. They would physically and spiritually die.

How long the two of them were frolicking around buck naked, singing, laughing, playing, working and communing with God before Satan appeared the bible is silent on. Satan would soon appear and he would tempt, deceive and ultimately wreck havoc on Adam, Eve and every human being that would be born in the history of civilization. Besides being one of the most powerful angels in existence, Satan was at the top of the ladder when it came to wisdom and beauty. Here is what the bible says in describing him. *"You were the model of perfection, full of wisdom and perfect in beauty. You were in Eden, the garden of God; every precious stone adorned you; ruby, topaz and emerald, chrysolite, onyx and jasper, sapphire, turquoise and beryl. Your settings and mountings were made of gold; on the day you were created they were prepared. You were anointed as a guardian cherub, for so I ordained you. You were on the holy mount of God; you walked among the fiery stones. You were blameless in your ways from the day you were created till wickedness was found in you." Ezek 28:12-15*

Satan walked with God and talked with God in the royal throne room at the center of the universe and was the arguably the greatest creature of God's creation as he was described as 'the model of perfection'. That changed when Satan with his free will decided that it was not enough to live in the splendor of heaven and serve and worship the one on the throne. It was he who should be on the throne and he convinced 1/3 of the angels to join his rebellion.

Whether God snapped his fingers, yelled the word 'NO', or did something else, the revolt was squashed. Satan and his partners in crime were banished from heaven and were given a death sentence. At the end of God's plan with humanity on earth Satan and the other fallen angels will be tossed into the lake of fire that God created for them to suffer for all of eternity. Their crime of rebellion that they committed is unforgiveable because they had lived with and communed with their creator on the highest level of intimacy possible. My guess to why Satan thought he had a chance was because he thought God was weak. Sin had not existed until Satan birthed it in his mind, so Satan had never seen God show his holy hate of sin, his holy justice towards sin, and his omnipotent power to immobilize it and remove it from his presence. The bible does not say when this happened but I believe that this happened not to long after Adam and Eve were created.

Adam and Eve were made in the image of God and were designed to be superior in essence and role over the community of angelic beings. Besides wanting to replace God on the throne, as it is written in Isaiah 14:12-14, I believe Satan was extremely envious of these two new beings made in the image of God. They would supplant him in honor, and his pride could not accept it. So sometime in the garden before the first of their many, many, many children were born, Satan came to deceive Adam and Eve, destroy their relationship with God and try to ruin the grand plan of God. There is much that can be said about this narrative in Genesis 3 but I will just point out one thing; Satan lied. The draw or carrot that he dangled in front of them was what he actually wanted for himself, and that was they could be like God. The appeal to deity, self autonomy, no accountability and power had sucked them in. He told them that they would become like God if they ate from the tree that God said they should not eat from. They believed the lie, questioned the sincerity of God and ate from the tree.

After Adam and Eve ate from the tree their spiritual DNA was altered and they were now no longer holy. The human race was now contaminated with the spiritual disease called sin which kills both the body and the soul. They both began their descent down the slippery slope in the 'valley of physical decay' towards deaths door. The physical body now had a time clock that counted down to their last breath and then the grave. The other death was and is spiritual death. This death breaks connection with the source of our spiritual life which is God himself. The plug that goes into the power source was figuratively pulled out. A fish lives in water; once you take the fish out of its life sustaining environment it will eventually die. So is the case for man.

Because of the broken relationship and because of God's deep love he made a provision for mankind to reconnect with him. What he did will come later, first I will tell you who he is.

Who is God? Let us start out by saying who God is not. He is not a cosmic Santa Claus who responds to our selfish wants or is obligated to give us something because we prayed some type of religious formula. The bible is very clear that God hears all prayers and answers all prayers. The answer to our prayers maybe no and/or delayed because He answers in his timeframe and not in ours. Also, the means to the outcome and the outcome can be different than what we wanted or could have happily imagined. Some people suggest that God is a distant being who watches from afar and does not involve himself in the affairs of this world. Tell that to the people he has restored eyesight to, cured lameness, delivered from demonic possession, delivered from addictions, saved marriages and other relationships, removed depression, and forgave the guilt of sin and they and I will just laugh.

Lastly he is not like those powerful make believe beings we see on Star Trek or other television shows or movies. Those depictions of God are everything a God created in man's image would be like. They can be manipulated by a more cunning man, are impulsive, dabble in the follies of man, are malicious, and have no concept of humility. They believe truth is relative and man can become a God as well through self awareness, time and experience. This alone would be proof in its self that the God of the bible is the one and true God because he doesn't fit in the thinking and imagination of man. Yes he is omnipotent, omniscient, and omnipresent but he also has innate qualities that are foreign to man's thinking and action. Who would voluntarily suffer and die a humiliating death for their enemy? The answer is nobody except Jesus. Who would patiently wait decades and scores of years for a person to stop sinning against them, instead of giving them their deserved penalty when they have the power and authority to do so? The answer is nobody except Jesus. God's love is beyond comprehension that he would do this for the whole world including those who hate him.

No human would create a God like that, because it would be seen as weak and is contraire to the unholy heart of man. What person has not thought about what they would do if they were God? I won't tell you how many people I killed when I imagined I was God. How dare you not allow me to merge into traffic! Zap, you are dead. Thank goodness God is not like us, or else we all would have been zapped along time ago.

Jesus asked the disciples who they think he is. At the beginning of his ministry they were unsure. After three years of watching him do things and say things that were above and beyond human abilities and never once sinning, they concluded that he was the promised messiah of the Old Testament. He was God come to earth to save mankind. Who you say Jesus is will be the most important question you will ever face in all of eternity. *"I am the Way, the Truth and the Life; no one goes to the Father except through me."*

John 14:6

Our enemy

Standing in the way of us finding out who we are and who God is, are Satan and the 1/3 of the angels we now call demons. Demons know the word of God frontwards and backwards. They twist the truth, are incomplete with the truth, and have inspired mankind to create false alternatives to God's truth of the bible. Demons are not pretend beings that are a symbolic representation of evil. Writers of the old and New Testament attest to the actual reality of their existence. Most importantly Jesus affirmed their existence by casting them out of people, stopping their actions and verbally speaking about their unbridled hate for all of the inhabitants on planet earth. Jesus said that they can only do what he allows and at the end of God's timetable of redemption, they will all be tossed into the Lake of Fire to be tormented forever.

Demons are not to be toyed with or underestimated. They have superhuman strength, are extremely intelligent, and have great powers. They have lived through all of mankind's history and are totally tuned into our weaknesses in general as well as individually. Demons oppose the plans of God, promote false religions, can afflict people with physical maladies, influence people to pervert what is good and right, tempt people to do wrong, and can enter into a person and take control. All people have been and can be influenced by demons. Their ability to damage and/or influence is diminished proportionately to the amount of belief and obedience a person demonstrates in regards to the bible. They have a deep hate for God, the bible, and anyone who reads, believes and obeys the bible.

What God Did

The bible is not a book of rules for human behavior. It is above all a record of the great saving acts of God. God has acted toward man in a way that demands a human response. No one can understand what he must do unless he first understands what God has done. When sin entered the world, God's justice declared death as the only viable means of appeasement. The penalty of sin however small warrants death. The sacrificial system was established to remind people that the sacrificed animal was a substitute for them. This sacrificial system was set up by God to be temporary until Jesus would come down from heaven to be the ultimate, complete and forever sacrifice for the whole world. The Old Testament had an example of this found in the Passover. This was also symbolic of what Jesus would do about 1500 years later.

God instructed all of the Israelites to sacrifice an unblemished lamb (Jesus was unblemished and had no sin) and apply the blood of the lamb on the door posts of all the households. All who trusted God did this. The angel of death came and swept through all of Egypt and killed the first born of every family who did not have their door posts covered with blood. Everyone who trusted and obeyed was protected. *"The blood will be a sign for you on the houses where you are; and when I see the blood, I will Passover you." (Exodus 12:13)*

Jesus was the perfect and all all-encompassing Lamb of God whose blood would be sufficient for all people for all time. Because of his death and the shedding of his blood he has made salvation possible and available to all who ask. When a person believes in Jesus and accepts his sacrifice on behalf of them, they are looked upon by God as having the blood of Jesus on the door of their heart and God's judgment will 'Passover' them.

Besides salvation, Jesus also gives healing to the many problems mankind has become victim to. He transforms and fixes people's broken lives. He heals depression, breaks the addiction to drugs, alcohol or other destructive vices, turns a thief into a giver, turns a hater into a lover, restores broken relationships and gives peace, joy, thankfulness and contentment to all that love him. He makes us a new person and allows us to have a better life. What Jesus did for all of humanity by dying on the cross are found in these three verses:

- *"For God so loved the world that anyone who believes in Him will not perish but will have eternal life." Jn 3:16*
- *"Therefore, if anyone is in Christ, he is a new creation; the old has gone, the new has come!" 2Cor 5:17*
- *"I have come that they may have life, and have it to the full." Jn 10;10*

    What Jesus has done, does and will do is more than I can possible write. He entered our world to save us, change us and allow us to experience life in a more meaningful and deeper way.

Why God Did It

What would prod the ruler of the universe in the greatest of humility to come down from heaven to be born in a stable? Why would he (Jesus) tolerate and allow at all, men to spit on him, mock him, beat him, stab him in the side with a spear, and finally hang on a cross to die? LOVE!! Another facet on the diamond of God's personality is his holy justice. This is another reason why he did what he did on the cross. The bible says that the ten commandments and other laws and regulations were given to us to show that we are sinners in need of a savior. The laws cannot intrinsically change us, they only make us guilty. As seen with Adam and Eve, God's justice cries out for even one sin committed.

Sin however small is an offense that deserves the maximum penalty when it is understood and seen through the lens of a holy God. Since there is nothing we can give or do to satisfy the righteous demands of a holy God, he made the provision for us. Jesus' death on the cross satisfied those righteous demands; the just for the unjust.

If this next reason why he did what he did does not excite you then check your pulse, you might not be alive. He did what he did to open up the door for all believers to become his adopted children and live with him for all of eternity in paradise with their changed hearts and minds that think and act like Jesus. Everyone will experience and give perfect love, have pure peace and full joy for ever with God without interruption. Wow!

Our Response

The bible is God's love letter to humanity begging the world to repent and be saved. There is only one way to heaven and it is through Jesus. Getting wet as a baby and/or being a member of a church is not sufficient. The ONLY thing that God accepts is faith in Jesus. C.S. Lewis said it simply but profoundly. Jesus is either a liar, a lunatic, or he is Lord. If he is not a liar or a lunatic then the only thing left is Lord. If he is Lord, and it has already been established that he loves you so much that he would die for you, what should your response be?

Tell Jesus thank you for dying on the cross in your place. Tell him that you are tired of living in the gray of life. Ask him to please forgive you of your sins and that you recognize him as the savior of your soul. Ask him to come into your life as Lord.

Start reading the bible and find a good church to help you grow. And lastly, smile, smile, smile, because your life of gray is about to end.

"No eye has seen, no ear has heard, no mind has conceived what God has prepared for those who love him." 1Corinthians 2:9

God bless you!!
Wade Oliver

ABOUT THE AUTHOR

Wade Oliver is married and has three adult children, one dog and one very demanding cat. He lives in Robbinsdale, Mn. and works for the USPS in Minneapolis, Mn.